# Should I Start A Podcast? What About!!??! A Step by Step Guide to Achieving Your Podcasting Dream

Jennifer Boyte

Published by Aspire Publishing, 2024.

SHOULD I START A PODCAST? WHAT ABOUT!!??! A STEP BY STEP GUIDE TO ACHIEVING YOUR PODCASTING DREAM

**First edition. May 26, 2024.**



ISBN: 979-8224377954

Written by Jennifer Boyte.

# Also by Jennifer Boyte

Procrastination No More: The Ultimate Guide To Boosting Productivity And Achieving Your Goals
Goal Mastery: A Practical Guide To Setting And Achieving Your Dreams
Should I Start A Podcast? What About!!??! A Step by Step Guide to Achieving Your Podcasting Dream

## Introduction: Unveiling the Podcasting Dream

Hey there, future podcasting superstar! Are you ready to embark on an incredible journey that will transform your life and help you achieve your wildest dreams? Well, buckle up, buttercup, because we're about to dive into the wonderful world of podcasting!

First things first, let's address the elephant in the room. You might be thinking, "Should I really start a podcast? I mean, isn't everyone and their grandma doing it these days?" The answer is a resounding YES! But here's the thing: not everyone is doing it right, and that's where you come in.

Starting a podcast is like having a heart-to-heart with your best friend, except instead of just one friend, you've got a whole bunch of them tuning in from all over the world. It's a chance to share your passions, your stories, and your unique perspective with a community of like-minded individuals who are eager to learn and grow with you.

Now, I know what you might be thinking. "But I'm just a small business owner/creative person/[insert your amazing identity here]. What do I have to offer?" Let me tell you, my friend, you have everything to offer! Your experiences, your challenges, and your triumphs are all valuable lessons that can inspire and motivate others who are walking a similar path.

But before we get ahead of ourselves, let's talk about the elephant in the room: procrastination. As a world-renowned author and expert on the subject, I've seen firsthand how procrastination can hold us back from pursuing our dreams. It's like having a mischievous little gremlin sitting on your shoulder, whispering sweet nothings about Netflix binges and social media scrolling.

But fear not, my dear friend! We're going to tackle this beast head-on and show that gremlin who's boss. Throughout this book, we'll explore the psychological factors that contribute to procrastination and develop practical strategies to overcome them. We'll also delve into the world of time management and learn how to balance your podcasting passion with your other responsibilities, all while keeping the fun alive.

Speaking of fun, let's not forget why we're here: to create a podcast that not only entertains but also educates and inspires. We'll dive into the nitty-gritty of podcast creation, from choosing your niche to crafting compelling content that keeps your listeners coming back for more. And because I know you're a busy bee, we'll also explore ways to streamline your podcasting process and make it as efficient as possible.

But starting a podcast isn't all rainbows and butterflies. There will be challenges and pitfalls along the way, but don't worry – we've got you covered. We'll discuss common podcasting obstacles and provide you with the tools and strategies you need to overcome them. Whether it's dealing with technical difficulties or navigating the world of monetization, we'll be there every step of the way.

And because I know you're a hands-on learner, we'll be including plenty of exercises, worksheets, and reflection questions throughout the book. These interactive elements will help you apply what you've learned and take concrete steps toward achieving your podcasting dream.

So, my dear friend, are you ready to take the leap and start your podcasting journey? If you're nodding your head enthusiastically (or even if you're just nodding slightly), then let's get started! In the next chapter, we'll dive into the first step of creating your podcast: discovering your unique voice and niche.

But before we wrap up this chapter, I want you to take a moment and reflect on your podcasting dream. What does it look like? What kind of impact do you want to make? Take a few minutes to jot down your thoughts in the space below.

[Reflection space]

Remember, your dream is valid, and you have everything you need to make it a reality. So let's hop on this podcasting train together and see where it takes us!

Exercise:

1. Write down your top three reasons for wanting to start a podcast.
2. List any fears or doubts you have about starting a podcast and brainstorm ways to overcome them.
3. Identify three potential podcast topics that align with your passions and expertise.

See you in the next chapter, you podcasting rockstar!

# Chapter 1: What's All the Buzz About Podcasts?

What is a podcast, anyway? Imagine if radio had a baby with on-demand streaming, and that baby was raised on a steady diet of diverse topics ranging from soap-making to quantum physics. That's a podcast! It's like having a buffet of audio content at your fingertips, ready to be devoured whenever and wherever you please.

A podcast is essentially a series of spoken-word episodes that you can download or stream from the internet. They can vary in length, from bite-sized nuggets of wisdom to epic sagas that rival the duration of your last Monday meeting (you know, the one that could've been an email). The beauty of podcasts lies in their accessibility and versatility. Anyone with a microphone and something to say can create one, making it a platform for entrepreneurs to share industry insights, influencers to connect with their audience on a deeper level, and creative folks to find their tribe of niche enthusiasts.

Whether you're an aspiring business mogul looking for tips on scaling your startup or a cat-loving knitting enthusiast seeking like-minded individuals, there's a podcast out there for you. And the best part? You can tune in whenever and wherever you want, whether you're stuck in traffic, burning dinner, or pretending to pay attention during a Zoom meeting. Podcasts are like your new best friend who always has something interesting to say, but in a pre-recorded, highly curated way.

Why do people love podcasts so much? In today's fast-paced world, who has the time to sit down and read a book? (Okay, maybe you do, but let's pretend you don't for the sake of this argument.) Podcasts have become the ultimate multitasking companion, allowing you to absorb knowledge and entertainment while going about your daily life. Imagine transforming mundane tasks like commuting, cleaning, or scrolling through social media into opportunities for personal growth and inspiration. It's like having a portable, on-demand university in your pocket!

One of the reasons podcasts have skyrocketed in popularity is the sheer variety of content available. There's literally something for everyone, from business advice and true crime stories to comedy shows and everything in between. It's like walking into an all-you-can-eat buffet for your brain – you can sample a little bit of everything until you find the perfect flavors that satisfy your intellectual cravings.

Can I really start my own podcast? Absolutely, you can! And guess what? You don't need a fancy studio or a team of audio engineers to make it happen. The beauty of podcasting lies in its low barrier to entry. If you have a phone, some basic recording equipment (which can be as simple as a smartphone and a quiet room), and a passion for sharing your ideas with the world, you're already halfway there!

Now, I know what you might be thinking: "But I don't have a huge following or any experience in broadcasting!" Fear not, my friend. Many successful podcasters started with an audience of just their mom, their best friend, and maybe their pet goldfish. The key is to start somewhere and allow your podcast to grow organically.

First things first, you'll want to zero in on your podcast idea. What topics set your soul on fire? What unique perspectives or experiences can you bring to the table? Remember, your podcast doesn't have to appeal to everyone – it just needs to resonate with your target audience. Once you've nailed down your concept, it's time to start planning your first episode.

Don't put too much pressure on yourself to create the perfect script or have all the answers right away. Some of the most engaging moments in podcasts are the authentic, unscripted ones – the laughter, the tangents, and the "aha!" moments that come from genuine conversation. Start with a rough outline to keep you on track, but allow room for spontaneity and personality to shine through.

And if the thought of diving into the technical aspects of podcasting makes you feel like you're drowning in a sea of jargon, don't worry! We'll break it down into manageable steps and provide you with the tools and resources you need to navigate this exciting new world.

So, are you ready to join the podcasting revolution? Get ready to unleash your voice, share your story, and connect with an audience that's eager to hear what you have to say. In the next chapter, we'll dive deeper into crafting your podcast identity and defining your niche. But for now, take a moment to reflect on the possibilities that await you on this thrilling journey.

Reflection Questions:

1. What topics or themes do you feel most passionate about sharing with others?
2. What unique experiences, skills, or perspectives do you bring to the table that could set your podcast apart?
3. Who is your ideal listener, and what value can you provide them through your podcast?

Let's get ready to embrace the power of podcasting and embark on an adventure filled with creativity, connection, and endless opportunities for growth. Your voice matters, and the world is waiting to hear it!

# Chapter 2: Finding Your Podcast Niche

Identifying your passions and expertise Alright, it's time for a little soul-searching exercise that's actually fun! Imagine you're throwing a party, but not just any party – it's a Passion Party! The only things on the guest list are activities and subjects that make you feel like you've just had three espressos and won the lottery. So, what's playing on your Passion Party playlist? Maybe it's pottery, whipping up culinary masterpieces, coding, or even extreme ironing (yes, that's a real thing!).

Grab a pen and jot down everything that makes your heart sing. Don't hold back – this isn't the time to be practical. To really nail down what belongs at your Passion Party, think about those activities you can get lost in for hours without even realizing you've skipped a meal. Or consider those moments when you're so annoyingly cheerful that your friends have to remind you to stop talking about that thing because it's 3 a.m. and they need to sleep.

Once you've invited all your favorite activities to the party, it's time to send out the second batch of invitations – to your areas of expertise. What do you actually know something about? Think about what others say you're annoyingly good at or what skills make you the go-to person in a crisis. Are you the social media guru who can make a cat meme go viral? Or perhaps you're the whiz who can whip up restaurant-quality soufflés without breaking a sweat?

Remember, your expertise isn't limited to your professional life; it can include those quirky skills that make you the hero at family gatherings. Your step-by-step mastery in that obscure trivia game or your unparalleled ability to assemble IKEA furniture counts too! The point is to strike a harmonious balance between what lights up your soul and what you're really good at.

To put this into practice, start blending the two lists. If you love photography and you're a wizard with Instagram analytics, you might be the next influencer who combines stunning visuals with insightful data. The key is to identify overlaps where your passion meets your expertise – that's your sweet spot. Think of it like combining chocolate and peanut butter – awesome on their own, but dynamite together!

Researching existing podcasts in your niche Alright, fellow entrepreneurs, influencers, and creative minds, it's time to unleash your inner spy! Get ready to infiltrate the world of podcasting – think James Bond, but with a microphone. Before you dive headfirst into creating your podcast masterpiece, you need to see what's already out there. And by "see," I mean go on a full-on reconnaissance mission.

Start by browsing your favorite podcast platforms like Spotify, Apple Podcasts, or even that obscure one your hipster friend won't shut up about. Look for podcasts in your niche and take note of the heavy hitters. What are they doing right? More importantly, what could they be doing better? It's not stalking; it's strategic investigation. Yeah, let's call it that.

Next up: finding gaps in the market. You know, the opportunities where you can swoop in and save the day – or at least make some serious noise. When listening to these existing podcasts, pay attention to the content gaps. Are they all covering the same tired topics about entrepreneurship that were trendy back in 2015? Is there a serious lack of humor, relatable stories, or just downright interesting content? Basically, if you find yourself nodding off while they're talking, that's a golden opportunity for you.

Take notes – no, really, take notes! Write down what you like, what you hate, and what made you want to throw your phone at the wall. These are your clues, your gaps. After you've done your James Bond-level spying, it's time to brainstorm your unique twist. You're not just another cog in the podcasting machine; you're here to shine, and that gap you found? That's your spotlight.

Think about what makes you special. Is it your wild and crazy entrepreneurial journey, your ability to make even the driest business strategies sound intriguing, or your knack for making your audience feel like they're chatting with an old friend? Use those gaps to your advantage and plan your content accordingly. This isn't just about filling a need; it's about creating something so irresistibly engaging that your target audience can't help but tune in. Get ready, because your podcast isn't just going to enter the scene – it's going to take it by storm!

Narrowing down your topic and target audience Picture this: you're an archer at a medieval fair, trying to win the heart of a prince or princess. You've got your arrow nocked, bowstring taut, but instead of aiming, you just launch it into the woods hoping it'll hit something good. Spoiler alert: it won't. Precision shooting is all about focusing on that bullseye – much like narrowing down your podcast topic.

If you're an entrepreneur, a big part of winning over your audience (or investors) is showing that you know exactly what you're talking about, and you know it better than anyone else. Don't try to be a jack-of-all-trades; be the master of one. Imagine Shakespeare trying to write a chemistry textbook. Sure, it might be poetic, but nobody's passing Chem 101 with that.

Now, let's move on to identifying your tribe. Do you know who you're talking to? If not, it's like walking into a vegan potluck with a wagon full of ribs. Knowing your audience means understanding their needs, passions, and pet peeves. Whether you're addressing women entrepreneurs looking to break the glass ceiling or men searching for creative outlets outside the realm of sports, tailor your message to resonate with them.

Do some detective work. Stalk them on social media (in a non-creepy way, of course). What do they post about? What are they griping about? What memes are they sharing? Find your tribe and speak their language. If they're throwing around terms you don't understand, hit up Urban Dictionary and get in the loop!

Once you've hit your target with your topic and found the right people to talk to, you're halfway to running a kingdom. Narrowing down your topic and knowing your tribe means you can focus your efforts like a laser, making every word count. It's not about shouting from the rooftops hoping someone will hear; it's about having a cozy chat with people who actually care about what you have to say.

So, next time you pick up that metaphorical bow, remember: aim small, miss small, and always know who's listening. Your podcast niche is out there waiting for you – go find it and make it yours!

Reflection Questions:

1. What are your top three passions, and how can you incorporate them into your podcast?
2. What unique expertise or experiences do you have that could set your podcast apart from others in your niche?
3. Who is your ideal listener, and what specific problems or desires do they have that your podcast can address?

Now that you've got a better idea of your podcast niche, it's time to start crafting your podcast identity and planning your content. In the next chapter, we'll dive into the nitty-gritty of creating a brand that stands out and resonates with your target audience. Get ready to unleash your creativity and make your mark in the podcasting world!

Exercise:

� Brainstorm a list of 10 potential podcast topics based on your passions, expertise, and target audience.

� Research 3 existing podcasts in your chosen niche and identify what makes them unique and successful.

# Chapter 3: The Must-Have Equipment for Podcasting

Microphones, headphones, and audio interfaces Alright, folks. Let's talk about the mighty microphone. Imagine this: you're about to pour your heart out in a podcast, and your microphone is as effective as trying to have a conversation through a tin can and a string. Not ideal, right? Choosing the right microphone is crucial. Whether you're an entrepreneur pitching your next big idea, an influencer trying to sound divine, or just someone who wants to DIY their way into the next Grammy's, you need a mic that captures every glorious note of your voice.

Start with a condenser microphone, which loves those detailed vocal frequencies. If you're more budget-sensitive, a dynamic microphone won't shout as loud but still gets the job done. Think clear, think loud, and always make sure your mic isn't just a fancy doorstop.

Now, that brilliant voice needs some buddies—enter headphones and audio interfaces. Picture this: you're recording without headphones, and suddenly, an unexpected dog bark or mystery noise ruins your one perfect take. The agony! High-quality headphones are like your BFFs—they whisper sweet nothings of your audio intricacies right into your ears. Opt for over-ear, closed-back headphones to avoid leaking sound. Your ears—and your patience during editing—will thank you.

Let's not forget the unsung hero of this tech trio: the audio interface. These magical boxes turn your analog sound into digital delight, ensuring what you say is what they hear. USB audio interfaces are perfect for those dipping their toes in the tech pool; they're simple, effective, and won't ask for a prenup. For the savvy experts, a

Thunderbolt interface can carry more data at lightning speed, making even complex tracks smooth like butter. Ensure your interface has the right number of inputs and outputs—after all, no one needs the drama of wanting to add that extra microphone and finding no place to plug it in.

Recording and editing software Alright, budding entrepreneurs and influencers, let's talk about the battlefield of software options out there. You're standing in front of a digital buffet, but instead of food, it's a smorgasbord of apps, each claiming to be the best thing since gluten-free bread. Navigating this array of choices can feel like deciding whether to binge-watch that trending series or finally start that business plan. Spoiler: picking the right software is way more fun!

Adobe Audition, GarageBand, Audacity, oh my! It's like a game of marry, date, or dump, except you're committing more to your software than to your last Tinder match. If you're the type who dreams big, splurges on oat milk lattes, and practically lives on social media, Adobe Audition might be your soul software. It's the Beyoncé of editing tools—powerful, sophisticated, and a bit pricey. But hey, your audio will sound 'Flawless'.

If you're a Mac user who's reluctant to pay for streaming apps, meet GarageBand—your free personal recording studio. It's like that dependable friend who always shows up with a bottle of wine. It won't overwhelm you, but it'll get the job done with style. However, not to throw shade, but if you switch to Windows, it's ghosting you faster than a bad date.

And let's not forget about Audacity, the open-source software that's like the cool kid who doesn't care about labels. It's free, user-friendly, and works on both Mac and Windows. It might not have all the bells and whistles of its pricier counterparts, but it's perfect for beginners who want to dip their toes into the editing pool without drowning in complex features.

Creating a comfortable recording space Let's face it, as an entrepreneur, influencer, or someone with a burning desire to create, your podcasting throne should rival that of any monarch. Your chair is your throne, and it needs to be as comfy as a cloud, yet supportive enough that you don't start resembling the Hunchback of Notre-Dame after a few recording sessions. Think ergonomic, padded just right, and adjustable in more ways than a Swiss Army knife. If your chair doesn't already make you feel like you're attending a high-stakes board meeting while wrapped in a warm hug, it's time for an upgrade. A throne fit for a podcasting king or queen can make all the difference. Your spine, and your listeners, will thank you when you're not shifting around like you sat on Captain Hook's hook.

Soundproofing is crucial, not just because you don't want to share your hot takes on entrepreneurial success with your chatty neighbor next door, but because outside noise can turn your podcast into a comedy of errors. Invest in some acoustic panels; they're those fancy foam pieces that look like egg cartons graduated from design school. Stick them on your walls like you're wallpapering with modern art. If you're on a budget, thick curtains or even the cozy comfort of your childhood blanket fort can work wonders. Basically, you want to transform your recording space into the Batcave of sound, where no unwanted noise can intrude.

Think about what makes you comfortable, beyond just your chair. Have a table that keeps everything within arm's reach so you're not flailing around like you're playing an invisible game of whack-a-mole. A good set of headphones is non-negotiable too—ones that fit snugly and don't make your ears feel like they just participated in an endurance marathon. And let's not forget hydration. Keep a stealthy water bottle on hand. Yeah, it's not a scepter, but a well-hydrated voice is a happy voice.

Remember, your recording space is your sanctuary, your creative oasis. Make it a place where you feel inspired, comfortable, and ready to unleash your inner podcasting rockstar. With the right equipment and a space that feels like home, you'll be well on your way to creating a podcast that's as unique and captivating as you are.

Reflection Questions:

1. What type of microphone best suits your recording needs and budget?
2. Which recording and editing software do you feel most comfortable using, and why?
3. How can you optimize your recording space to ensure the best possible sound quality?

In the next chapter, we'll dive into the art of crafting compelling podcast content that keeps your listeners hooked and coming back for more. Get ready to flex your creative muscles and make some serious podcast magic!

Exercise:

� Create a shopping list of the essential podcasting equipment you need based on your budget and recording setup.

� Practice setting up and testing your equipment to ensure optimal sound quality.

# Chapter 4: Crafting Compelling Content

Developing engaging topics and episode formats Listen up, all you aspiring content moguls out there. We're talking entrepreneurs hustling from dawn till the next caffeine hit, influencers counting likes like they're lottery tickets, and anyone else who thinks a microphone is more than just a tool for karaoke night. We're diving into the wild, wonderful world of creating engaging topics and episode formats. Because seriously, no one wants to listen to you drone on about your cat's dietary habits unless it has a twist like, I don't know, your cat runs a thriving vegan bakery on the side.

First, let's talk topics. Be bold, be different, be that person everyone talks about at the water cooler with a mixture of envy and admiration. The world does not need another generic "How to Be Productive" episode. We need "How to Be Productive While Going Down a Rabbit Hole of Cat Memes." You have to find that angle that makes people think, "Wow, this person gets me, and also, this is hilarious." Whether you're targeting female entrepreneurs balancing empires and diapers, or men figuring out how to turn their mid-life crises into mid-life victories, you need a hook. And it better be sharp.

Now let's get jazzy with formats. One-size-fits-all might work for socks, but not for episode structures. Interviews are super popular, but here's the real tea: everyone does them. Mix it up! Think beyond the basic question-answer routine. Try "hot take" segments where guests get sixty seconds to rant about industry pet peeves. How about a game show format where influencers compete in ridiculous challenges tied to their niche? Or maybe an advice column where viewers submit the weirdest, wackiest questions and you try to answer them seriously, while keeping a straight face and a laugh track in your heart.

Your format should reflect your personality. Are you sarcastic and edgy? Go for a format that lets you inject your snark. Are you warm and fuzzy? Opt for a storytelling format, but add a quirky twist, like narrating the whole thing as if it's an epic bedtime story. Your audience isn't just sticking around for your content; they're sticking around for your unique voice. And remember, do all this while making sure your grandma could follow your content. Simplicity is key, but simplicity doesn't have to be boring.

In the end, the ultimate hack: trial and error. Test different topics and formats, look at the engagement data, and listen to your audience. They are basically your second-in-command (besides your cat baker) when it comes to what works and what flops. Adapt, pivot, and strut down the creative runway with your newfound content swagger.

Interviewing techniques and guest selection Let's face it, interviewing is an art form. Oprah didn't become a legend by asking boring questions. She knows how to dig deep and get people talking. As an entrepreneur or influencer, you have to channel your inner Oprah. Start with open-ended questions. This isn't a court hearing, so steer clear of anything that can be answered with a plain "yes" or "no." Instead of asking, "Do you like your job?" try something like, "What inspired you to pursue your career?" This approach opens the door for your guest to walk through and spill the juicy details.

Silence is your friend. Awkward pauses? They're not awkward—they're golden! People get uncomfortable with silence and tend to fill the void. Often, they offer some of the most insightful information during these moments. So, throw that pause around like you're tossing confetti at a New Year's Eve party. Eye contact is crucial too. Don't stare into their souls (because creepy), but let them know you're listening. Nod, lean in slightly, or give a little "mmm-hmm" now and then. It's like sprinkling a bit of magic dust on the conversation.

Choosing guests can feel like online dating. Swipe right on the ones who have value to offer your audience. Are they industry experts? Great side stories? Got some viral potential? In any case, your guests need to align with your brand. It's like finding the perfect dance partner—you don't want to cha-cha with someone whose idea of a good time is standing still.

Don't be afraid to dig into your network. That high school buddy who successfully started his own tech company might just be the ticket. And don't forget social media. It's a treasure trove of potential interviewees. Slide into those DMs like you're sliding down a rainbow. Personalize your message, explain why they'd be a great fit, and what's in it for them. Reciprocity is a fancy word for "scratch my back and I'll scratch yours," but it's a powerful approach.

Finally, always be prepared. Nothing screams unprofessionalism like a host who clearly hasn't done their homework. Brush up on your guest's background, recent projects, and any common interests you can mention. It's like preparing a marinade—the more you know, the tastier the conversation will be. And remember, just like a great recipe, it's all about balance. Frame your questions to keep things spicy without burning the dish. Happy interviewing!

Writing attention-grabbing episode titles and descriptions First impressions matter, especially when you're trying to grab someone's attention in a sea of content. Think of your episode title as the suitor dressed to impress, strutting down the content runway. It needs to turn heads, drop jaws, and make people pause their endless scrolling. Your title is the first step in this dance of seduction. An effective episode title does more than state its content; it's a blend of intrigue, wit, and promise. Avoid being as dull as a Monday morning meeting. Instead, aim for something that makes people click faster than they hit "snooze" on their alarms.

Never underestimate the power of the double entendre or a splash of humor. Titles like "Why Your Business is a Mess and How to Clean it Up Fast!" or "The Tweeting Peacock: Master Social Media Without Losing Your Feathers" mix clarity with curiosity. Be specific yet enticing. You want your audience to know there's something in it for them, but also hint at some fun along the way. The aim is to excite the entrepreneurs, influencers, and creative minds that you're targeting. A great title is like a promise of value wrapped up in a delightful mystery.

Once your audience is hooked by the title, the next step is keeping them engaged with your episode description. The episode description should flirt with your potential listeners, giving them just enough to leave them eager for more. Keep it concise but powerful. If your episode was a movie, the description would be the trailer—full of highlights, a few teasing snippets, and a sprinkle of suspense. Drop tantalizing hints about the juicy bits to come without giving away the plot. Remember, leaving some elements to the imagination is part of the chase. A dash of humor and a sprinkle of excitement can turn a simple description into an irresistible invitation. As with great flirtation, the art lies in balancing revelation and mystery.

The ultimate goal is to make your episode stand out in a crowded digital space. You want your title and description to be the shiny objects that catch your audience's eye and refuse to let go. Remember, you're not just competing with other podcasts; you're competing with a million other distractions. Your title and description are your secret weapons in this battle for attention.

So, put on your creative cap, grab a pen (or a keyboard), and start brainstorming. Channel your inner Don Draper, minus the whiskey and existential crises. Play with words, experiment with different angles, and don't be afraid to push the envelope. The best titles and descriptions are the ones that make you a little nervous, the ones that feel just a bit daring.

And if you ever get stuck, just remember: what would your cat's vegan bakery do? Probably something unexpected, a little quirky, and undeniably irresistible. Let that be your guiding light as you craft the perfect titles and descriptions for your podcast episodes.

Reflection Questions:

1. What unique angle or perspective can you bring to your podcast topics to make them stand out?
2. How can you incorporate different episode formats to keep your content fresh and engaging?
3. What are some attention-grabbing title and description ideas for your upcoming episodes?

In the next chapter, we'll explore the technical side of recording and editing your podcast episodes. Get ready to put on your audio engineering hat and learn how to make your episodes sound like pure audio gold!

Exercise:

◈ Outline a sample episode for your podcast, including a catchy title, engaging intro, and key talking points.

◈ Record a 5-minute segment of your podcast and practice your storytelling and delivery skills.

# Chapter 5: Recording and Editing Like a Pro

Setting up your recording equipment Alright, future podcasting prodigies and YouTube sensations, let's dive headfirst into the wonderful world of setting up your recording equipment. Think of your recording gear as your biz partner in this creative venture. You've got the brains and charisma, and the equipment? Well, it better keep up. To kick things off, consider your microphone as your lifeline—your audio's BFF. It's like picking a life partner: choose wisely because the wrong one will just make you sound like you're talking through a 1980s payphone. Invest in a decent condenser microphone if you can swing it. Your audience's ears will thank you, and you can avoid that dreadful background noise that somehow equates to whales mating... in space.

Next up, headphones. Now, skip those cute little earbuds—unless your idea of adventure is torturing yourself with subpar audio. Grab a pair of over-ear, closed-back headphones. They're like those "Don't Disturb" signs, blocking out the world so you can focus entirely on the magic happening between you and your microphone. While we're at it, don't forget a pop filter. This nifty little accessory keeps your audio clear of those pesky plosives. No one wants to feel like they're abruptly living inside a popcorn machine every time you say a word starting with "p".

Ok, now that the basics are out of the way, let's connect everything without turning your workspace into the aftermath of a spaghetti factory explosion. Most modern setups will need an audio interface—kind of like a matchmaker for your microphone and computer. This bad boy converts your silky smooth voice into a digital format your computer can process. The key here is to follow the instruction manual. I know, wild concept. But avoid the temptation to speed-run through the setup and actually read those instructions. Your 10-year-old self who never read Lego instructions is probably screaming right now, but trust me, it's worth it. Once everything's connected, you're in the Business class, folks.

Now, before you start recording, take a moment to do a soundcheck. Put on those headphones and make sure everything sounds crystal clear. Adjust your microphone placement, fiddle with the gain settings, and do a quick test recording. Listen back and make sure there's no distortion, background noise, or any other audio gremlins trying to sabotage your setup. It's like checking your teeth for spinach before a big date—better safe than sorry!

Editing out mistakes and adding polish Alright folks, let's talk about the art of the snip snip. When it comes to creating a podcast, those pesky uhms and ahhs are the awkward uninvited guests that somehow snuck in. Snipping these out efficiently can transform your content from casual chit-chat to pro-level chatter. First up, embrace your inner ninja – be quick and precise. Listen through your recording and slice away those unnecessary pauses and fillers that add nothing but dead weight. Your audience doesn't need to hear you channel your inner caveperson, mumbling through thoughts.

But wait, don't get scissor-happy! It's crucial to maintain the natural flow. The aim is not to make it sound like a robot stitched together your sentences, but rather, that you're seamlessly eloquent. Take it slow, and use crossfade tools to smooth out any abrupt cuts. Think of it as blending a smoothie – you want a mix, not chunky bits of conversation interrupting the flow.

Now, onto giving it that extra sparkle – welcome to the polish party! This isn't about slapping on glitter, but rather fine-tuning your podcast to perfection. Start by levelling out volumes between different segments. Consistency is key, and nobody wants to adjust their volume dial constantly. Use noise reduction tools to zap away background noise. Yes, your neighbor's leaf blower doesn't need a cameo appearance.

For a more professional touch, add in musical intros and outros. But here's the kicker: make sure they align with your podcast's vibe. Avoid aggressive rock intros for a meditation podcast, unless you want your listeners jolting out of their Zen mode. Seamlessly integrate sound effects where necessary – just don't go overboard. Your podcast should be a symphony, not a noisy carnival ride.

Finally, listen to your podcast post-editing with fresh ears, or have someone else give it a whirl. This external feedback can highlight areas you might have missed and ensures your masterpiece is ready for the world. Remember, every great episode is made in the editing room, not just behind the mic!

Tips for creating professional-quality audio When it comes to audio, you absolutely cannot skimp on the basics. It's like trying to build a skyscraper with Jenga blocks — things can get wobbly real fast. Start with a decent microphone. Your laptop's built-in mic is great... if you're looking to record underwater. Investing in a USB microphone won't break the bank and will make you sound like a pro, even if you're recording in your PJs. Make sure you're in a quiet room; nobody wants to hear your neighbor's dog auditioning for American Idol while you're trying to drop some knowledge bombs.

Alright, now that we've cleared the basic audio hurdles, let's dive into the magic of sounding like a million bucks on a fistful of dollars. You'd think you need a soundproof studio and expensive gadgets, but even a closet stuffed with clothes can be an excellent recording space. Those clothes act like soundproofing panels for free. Add a pop filter to your mic setup to avoid sounding like you're launching spit missiles. And if you're feeling fancy, download free editing software like Audacity or

GarageBand; they're powerful enough to make you sound spectacular without turning your wallet into an echo chamber.

To add a cherry on top of your audio sundae, play around with equalization (EQ) settings. Boost the lows to give your voice depth like Morgan Freeman narrating your grocery list, and reduce high-frequency background noises. Experiment with different levels until your voice sounds crisp and full. And for the love of all things audio, normalize your audio levels to avoid blowing out eardrums or making people crank up the volume to hear you.

Lastly, the golden rule: always do a test recording before diving into your full episode. There's nothing worse than pouring your heart out for an hour, only to realize your mic was off, or you sound like you're speaking from the bottom of a well. Trust me, it's a mistake you only make once (or twice, if you're a slow learner like me).

Creating professional-quality audio doesn't have to be rocket science or cost you an arm and a leg. With a little know-how, some basic equipment, and a dash of creativity, you can have your listeners wondering if you've secretly built a state-of-the-art studio in your basement. And if they ask, just wink mysteriously and tell them it's all part of the magic of podcasting.

Reflection Questions:

1. What recording equipment do you currently have, and what upgrades might you need to improve your audio quality?
2. What editing techniques do you find most challenging, and how can you practice to improve your skills?
3. How can you optimize your recording space to achieve the best possible sound quality?

In the next chapter, we'll explore the world of podcast hosting and distribution. Get ready to learn how to get your podcast out into the world and into the ears of your eager listeners!

Exercise:

� Experiment with different microphone techniques and recording positions to find what works best for your voice and style.

� Edit a sample episode using your chosen software, focusing on removing filler words, adding transitions, and balancing audio levels.

# Chapter 6: Launching and Promoting Your Podcast

Choosing the right podcast hosting platform If you're diving into the exciting world of podcasting, think of your hosting platform like it's the fancy hotel where your audio genius checks in. You wouldn't want your precious episode stuck between the stairs and the elevator, right? Most definitely not! So, let's figure out where your podcast baby should find its nurturing home.

When it comes to platforms, there are a million and one choices out there. It's like a buffet, but instead of carbs and calories, you're navigating analytics, storage, and syndication options—yum! Alright, let's get real for a second. The top platforms each have their own bells and whistles, but if you're a budget-conscious newbie, you might want to consider something that offers a free tier. SoundCloud and Podbean are like the friendly neighbors who invite you over for a barbecue with no strings attached. But beware, free plans often come with limitations like storage caps and fewer features. They're the budget airlines of podcasting—just remember to bring your own peanuts.

If you're paying out of pocket (or passing off the bill to an enthusiastic sponsor), sites like Libsyn, Blubrry, or Anchor can give you more in terms of storage, powerful analytics, and additional tools for growth. Libsyn has been around since the dawn of podcasting time and is practically the granddaddy of podcast hosting. Blubrry offers not just hosting, but a neat WordPress plugin called PowerPress, making it easy to integrate your episodes directly into your blog. Anchor is like that trendy new café that lets you create, edit, and distribute all in one place, with monetization features right from the start.

Okay, let's cut to the chase—what's most important for you? If you're an entrepreneur wanting to drive business, analytics are your best friend. Want to be the next influencer? Then easy distribution across platforms will be a godsend. Have some super-exclusive content? Look for platforms that offer subscription models. When in doubt, write down what's crucial for you and compare platforms side-by-side. Nothing drives the point home like a good ol' pros and cons list made with lots of coffee and some inevitable hair-pulling.

Now, a golden nugget of wisdom: choose a platform that lets you keep control of your content. This is your podcast, your baby; you don't want some Big Brother platform dictating where your episodes can go or what they can say. Always read the fine print, possibly with a magnifying glass if your prescription's out of date. Remember, in the feast of podcast platforms, take what you need, leave what you don't, and always—always—get what works best for your unique flavor.

Ready to plant that podcast seed in fertile ground? Fantastic! With the right hosting platform, you'll have one less thing to worry about while you're busy becoming the next audio sensation.

Creating eye-catching cover art and branding Creating a podcast cover art that's eye-catching is like showing up to a networking event in a sequin jumpsuit – it's all about making a memorable first impression. Your podcast cover art is the first thing people see, so it needs to pop like a champagne bottle at a wedding. Think of it as the face of your podcast; it should embody your brand's personality without needing a second glance. Bright colors, bold fonts, and a catchy episode title can make your cover art instantly stand out among the sea of similar representations. Remember, a busy cover can make your art look like it got dressed in the dark. Clean, straightforward designs often communicate your podcast's theme more effectively, like a well-tailored suit at a business meeting.

Brand building isn't just about slapping a logo on your podcast cover and calling it a day. It's more like dating – you need to show your audience who you are before making any firm commitments. Every element of your brand, from the tone of your episodes to the colors in your logo, should scream you! Your brand should resonate with your target audience on a personal level. Are you the quirky, fun podcast that makes listeners LOL daily? Or are you the suave, professional show that teaches valuable business lessons? Keep consistency across all mediums – your website, social media, podcast episodes – because nobody likes dating someone who changes personalities every other date.

Entrepreneurs and influencers, take note: your podcast cover art should be as engaging as your last viral post. Women and men alike will engage more when your brand exudes confidence and reliability. For those looking for a creative outlet, think about what colors, fonts, and images represent the unique flair you bring to the mic. Keep experimenting until you find a combination that perfectly encapsulates the spirit of your podcast. And while you're at it, make sure your choices are readable and visually appealing even when shrunk down to thumbnail size. Trust us, nobody has time to squint at your artwork.

Final tip: Your cover art and branding should be a reflection of what listeners can expect from your content. So, if your podcast is all about quirky, off-the-wall content, make your cover art look like a circus tent. If it's a serious business podcast, aim for something sleek and professional. Remember, your branding goes beyond just the visual; it encompasses the way you communicate, the content you produce, and the relationship you build with your listeners. So, make it unforgettable in the best way possible.

Utilizing social media and other promotional strategies Let's dive into the wonderland of social media, where each platform is like its own themed party. Instagram is your bohemian brunch, Facebook is an office potluck, Twitter is a fast-food joint, and LinkedIn is, of course, a corporate gala. Oh, and don't forget TikTok, which is basically a non-stop dance-off. Now, instead of just attending these parties, you want to be the life of them, and more importantly, get everyone talking about you. Begin by defining your unique voice and vibe—it's like choosing your outfit. Are you the quirky person everyone remembers for your neon shoes, or the sophisticated one whose elegance is timeless?

Content is your secret weapon, so sprinkle it like confetti. Visual appeal is crucial. Let's be honest: no one's reading a novel on Instagram. Keep it snappy and visually pleasing. You don't need to be a professional photographer—your smartphone is good enough with some good lighting and a knack for composition. If visuals are the cake, then captions are the icing. Be relatable, be witty, and above all, be genuine. Authenticity resonates; think less robot, more human. Engage with your audience. Every comment is an opportunity to build a relationship. Like, reply, and make people feel seen.

Don't get stuck in the online world alone. There's a big, beautiful, physical realm out there. Guerrilla marketing is essentially pulling off the flash mobs of the marketing world. Unexpected, fun, and memorable. It could be as simple as wrapping your car with your brand colors or hosting an impromptu event in a public place. Combine this with your social media efforts by sharing these moments online, turning local buzz into actual buzzzzz.

Don't underestimate email marketing. Yes, it's as old as the Internet itself but consider it the bread-and-butter of your promotional sandwich. Personalization is key. Address your audience by their first name, share exclusive content, or give them special offers. Make them feel like they're part of an exclusive club with secret handshakes and everything. Tools like Mailchimp or Constant Contact make it easier than ever to create stunning emails without needing a degree in graphic design.

Finally, partnerships can be your best ally, like Batman and Robin. Look out for brands or individuals whose missions align with yours. Co-host events, collaborate on social media posts, or offer joint giveaways. Leveraging someone else's audience can dramatically expand your reach with minimal effort.

Remember, promoting your podcast is an ongoing process. It's not a "set it and forget it" kind of deal. Consistently engage with your audience, create valuable content, and always be on the lookout for new ways to spread the word about your audio masterpiece. And most importantly, have fun with it! Your enthusiasm will be contagious, and before you know it, you'll have a loyal army of listeners eagerly awaiting your next episode.

So, put on your marketing hat, grab your social media megaphone, and get ready to make some noise. Your podcast deserves to be heard, and with these promotional strategies in your toolkit, you'll be well on your way to building a thriving community of listeners who can't get enough of your unique voice and perspective.

Reflection Questions:

1. Which podcast hosting platform aligns best with your specific needs and goals?
2. How can you incorporate your unique personality and brand into your podcast cover art and overall branding?
3. What social media platforms and promotional strategies do you feel most comfortable using to promote your podcast?

In the next chapter, we'll explore the exciting world of monetizing your podcast and turning your passion into a profitable venture. Get ready to learn about sponsorships, affiliate marketing, and other creative ways to generate revenue from your podcasting efforts!

Exercise:

� Create a launch plan for your podcast, including a timeline, promotional content, and outreach strategies.

� Design eye-catching cover art and write a compelling description for your podcast.

# Chapter 7: Monetizing Your Podcast

Exploring sponsorship and advertising opportunities So you want someone to throw wads of cash at you just for existing? Welcome to the delightful world of sponsorships! It's no longer just for sports stars and movie legends; even your cat's Instagram account could land a sponsor. First thing's first: Define your worth and audience. Brands aren't in the business of charity; they want returns. Maybe your dog has the floppiest ears in the West or your YouTube channel reviews nail polish that glows in the dark. Find your unique angle—it's your golden ticket.

Now let's dive into the pitch. Keep it authentic! Even billion-dollar companies can smell a faker from a mile away. Talk about why you're a perfect match for their brand and throw in a sprinkle of what you can deliver—audience engagement, creative content, whatever you're good at. Top it off with stats, like your follower count or monthly views, because numbers talk faster than a politician at election time. Oh, and remember, don't beg. Confidence is your best friend here.

Shall we move to adverts? This isn't about plastering PDFs on every possible surface of your content. Ads should feel as natural as avocado on toast. You want them to blend seamlessly with your style so your audience doesn't hit "skip" faster than you can say "ROI." Whether it's a clever podcast plug or a quirky YouTube pre-roll, keep it fun, engaging, and oh-so-you.

Consider your platform's algorithm like that one quirky friend who only hooks you up with people you wouldn't dare swipe left on. Do a little research and find the best times to post content with integrated ads to maximize reach. And hey, know your worth because if a deal sounds too good to be true, it probably is. Usage rights matter; you don't want your face selling lawnmowers in another continent without your consent.

When it comes to sponsorships and advertising, it's all about finding the right fit. Look for brands that align with your values and resonate with your audience. You don't want to be promoting a meat-lover's pizza if your podcast is all about veganism (unless you're into some serious irony). And don't be afraid to get creative with your ad integrations. A well-placed sponsor shoutout or a clever product tie-in can make your listeners chuckle while still getting the message across.

Setting up a Patreon or other crowdfunding options Imagine your fan base throwing digital dollar bills at you, cheering you on, and financing your creative ventures. Yes, it's possible! With platforms like Patreon, Kickstarter, or GoFundMe, you can get funded by your die-hard supporters. First things first, give them a reason to invest in you. Create engaging content that makes them go, "Hey, I'd totally pay for this!" Before you know it, you'll be swimming in coffee money (and let's face it, probably real money too).

Setting up a Patreon involves a few steps that are as easy as spreading butter on toast – just less messy. Sign up, create a compelling profile that screams, "I'm worth it!", and set up your tiers. Tiers are levels of support that offer different rewards. Make them enticing, like exclusive content, early access, or behind-the-scenes bloopers that are too hilarious to keep to yourself. A secret squirrel selfie? Why not!

Don't just stop at Patreon if it's not your jam. Explore other crowdfunding options. Kickstarter is for project-based campaigns – perfect for launching that snazzy new invention or publishing your memoirs at the tender age of 25. Make sure your campaign is engaging and visually appealing. High-quality images and a video where you're enthusiastically convincing people why funding you is the best decision they'll make all week can work wonders.

GoFundMe is the platform for personal causes, where stories tug at heartstrings and people donate out of the kindness of their hearts. It's a softer approach to crowdfunding, usually employed for personal projects or support. Be honest, transparent, and as personable as your friendly neighborhood cat video curator. And remember, all these platforms thrive on sharing and caring – spread the word and watch the funds roll in.

Before you dive in, keep these golden rules in mind: be genuine, offer real value, and stay engaged with your supporters. Respond to their comments, thank them profusely, and maybe even throw in the occasional "thank you" video where you sing their praises – literally, if you're up for it. Your supporters are more likely to feel connected and continue their support if they see the real you, warts and all.

Crowdfunding can be a fantastic way to build a community around your podcast while also generating some much-needed funds to keep the show running. Just remember, it's not a one-and-done deal. Consistently deliver value to your supporters, keep them in the loop about your progress, and show your appreciation for their generosity. Who knows, you might just find yourself with a loyal army of superfans who can't wait to see what you create next!

Creating products and services related to your podcast Imagine you have a thriving community hanging on to your every word. What's next? Simple—sell them stuff! But not just any stuff, mind you. We're diving into merch madness, so think about things your listeners would actually love. Ever wondered why every successful podcast seems to have a snazzy t-shirt, a funky mug, or an adorable sticker? It works. Picture your listeners sipping coffee from a mug with your logo every morning. Now, merch isn't limited to just t-shirts and mugs. Consider posters with memorable quotes from your show, or tote bags for the eco-friendly crowd. Think about what resonates with your audience and get creative. Who wouldn't want to wear your podcast's punniest catchphrase on a hoodie?

Speaking of extensions, let's pivot to courses, ebooks, and the like. Imagine your podcast is about leading a healthier lifestyle. You can whip up an ebook packed with tips, recipes, and workout routines. Or maybe you're a digital marketing guru—you could create a course showing listeners how to turn their blog into a moneymaking machine. The trick is to expand on what you're already doing well. If your episode on mastering social media got rave reviews, a detailed ebook diving deeper into that topic could be a hit. Extensions let you dive into the nitty-gritty while offering immense value. They can be a great way to establish yourself as not just a podcaster, but an authority in your field.

To squash your doubts, let's see how to implement this easily. Start small. Maybe launch a limited edition t-shirt or a short, simple ebook. Platforms like Teespring for merch or Gumroad for digital products make this a breeze. Tie these launches with special episodes announcing your new product. Offer something exclusive for your top fans; a little VIP treatment goes a long way. Keep an eye on what sells and be prepared to pivot. If tote bags are flying off the shelves but the beanies you launched are gathering dust, adjust accordingly. The aim is to dip your toes into the merch and product world before diving headfirst.

Remember, your products and services should be an extension of your podcast's brand and message. They should provide additional value to your listeners and help them dive deeper into the topics you cover. And don't be afraid to get feedback from your audience. Ask them what kind of products they'd like to see or what topics they'd love to learn more about in an ebook or course.

Creating products and services related to your podcast can be a fun and rewarding way to monetize your efforts while also strengthening your connection with your listeners. Plus, there's nothing quite like the feeling of seeing someone rocking your podcast's logo on a t-shirt or hearing about how your ebook changed someone's life. So, get those creative juices flowing and start brainstorming some killer product ideas!

Reflection Questions:

1. What unique value can you offer potential sponsors or advertisers, and how can you pitch your podcast effectively?
2. Which crowdfunding platform aligns best with your goals, and what rewards can you offer your supporters?
3. What products or services could you create that would provide additional value to your listeners and align with your podcast's brand?

In the next chapter, we'll dive into the world of podcast analytics and how to measure your success. Get ready to learn about download numbers, listener engagement, and other key metrics that can help you fine-tune your podcasting strategy and keep your audience coming back for more!

Exercise:

⯑ Research potential sponsors or advertisers in your niche and craft a sample pitch email.

⯑ Brainstorm 3 product or service ideas related to your podcast that you could develop and sell to your audience.

# Chapter 8: Overcoming Common Podcasting Challenges

Dealing with audio quality issues Sound snafus can turn your grand audio dreams into a nightmarish symphony of crackles, pops, and the dreadful tin-can effect. If you're an entrepreneur, an influencer, or someone diving into a creative project where pristine sound is a must, encountering audio issues is like finding a fly in your soup—it's frustrating, gross, and entirely avoidable with the right tricks up your sleeve.

First off, let's talk about the infamous audio buzz. This little gremlin usually creeps in because of electrical interference or shoddy equipment. If your microphone is picking up enough background noise to resemble a bee hive, try separating your audio cables from power cables—these two get along about as well as cats and dogs. Also, ensure that your equipment is properly grounded. Nobody wants to listen to your electrifying karaoke session, no matter how impressive your vocal range might be.

Then there's the dreaded echo. Imagine talking to someone who insists on repeating every word you say—it's fun for about three seconds. Echo in your audio recordings happens for similar reasons. Hard surfaces—like concrete walls, tiles, and glass—love to bounce sound back. To combat this, create a make-shift sound booth using anything soft and fluffy. Pile up those pillows and mount blankets around your recording area. You might feel like you're camping in your living room, but your listeners will thank you for it.

Now, about that pesky background noise—birds chirping, dogs barking, and your neighbor deciding to host a drum circle right when you hit the record button. Good news: this can be zapped out with noise reduction software. Invest in a decent audio editing tool that has noise reduction features, and use it like you're sprinkling magic dust over your recording. Just remember, with great power comes great responsibility; too much noise reduction can make your voice sound as if you're speaking from inside a fish tank.

Practice makes perfect, but preparation prevents a lot of hefty post-production work. Always do a test recording before diving into the real thing. Clap your hands or make some noise just to see if your setup picks up anything unwanted. Adjust accordingly before pouring your heart out into the microphone. Trust us, future you will be eternally grateful.

Where's the silver lining in this cloud of sound snafus? Knowledge. Understanding these common issues means you're halfway to becoming an audio wizard. By dodging these usual suspects, your content will not only sound professional but will also ensure your audience stays hooked to every word.

Now, take this last piece of advice: always keep a backup recording. Tech gremlins are real, and they love to strike when you least expect it. A backup can save you from the agonizing cry of, "Oh no, it didn't record!" Embrace redundancy with open arms—it's your safety net in the audio jungle.

Remember, audio quality is a journey, not a destination. Even the most seasoned podcasters still encounter the occasional hiccup. The key is to learn from each mishap, refine your setup, and keep pushing forward. With persistence and a good sense of humor, you'll be well on your way to creating audio magic that'll make your listeners wonder if you've secretly set up shop in a professional recording studio.

Consistency and staying motivated Picture this: you're an entrepreneur or an influencer, and your audience eagerly awaits your next big move. Whether you're trying to revolutionize the world with the next killer app or sharing life-changing insights through your blog, consistency is your secret weapon. It's like flossing—not everyone does it, but those who do, well, they get to keep their teeth. So, how do you become a trusted part of your audience's routine without making them feel like they're stuck in a never-ending episode of a mundane soap opera?

First, set a realistic schedule. Don't promise your followers daily updates if you can barely manage bi-weekly without crying into your coffee. Start small. Aim for regularity rather than frequency. Kind of like sipping wine—better to have a glass every other night than two bottles in one evening. Use tools like content calendars or alarms on your phone. These are the little nudges that keep you on track.

Next, don't be afraid of repetition. If Coca-Cola can run the same ad a thousand times, you can certainly rehash key points in your content. Reemphasizing core ideas isn't lazy; it's smart. You're embedding your messages like those ridiculously catchy jingles that stick in your head forever. Consistency turns your brand into that reliable friend who's always there when you need them—minus the need for a lengthy therapy session afterward.

Now, onto keeping the spark alive. Motivation often feels like your last Tinder date—hot and heavy one moment, ghosting you the next. You need to keep it fresh and exciting, like a romantic first date with your audience, every single time. Here's a hot tip: variety is the spice of life. If you're always serving Caesar salad, eventually people will crave a burger. Throw in different types of content—videos, blogs, podcasts, or even an entertaining meme now and then. The element of surprise keeps everyone hooked.

Remember your "Why". Why did you start this journey in the first place? Was it the thrill of entrepreneurship, the joy of sharing your passions, or maybe just figuring out how to avoid working a 9-5? Write that reason down and stick it somewhere visible, like your desk or, heck, even your fridge. Every glance becomes a gentle reminder, like your phone's step counter urging you to take those 10,000 steps you promised yourself you'd take.

Surround yourself with motivators. Friends, colleagues, or even a particularly inspiring cat video can help. We're social creatures, and motivation is contagious. Hang out with people who push you to be better. Even when your best laid plans of mice and men seem to go awry, these motivators keep you in the game.

Finally, reward yourself. Achieving small milestones should be reason enough to treat yourself. Finished a month of consistent posts? Toast yourself with a fancy glass of your favorite beverage or take a day off doing absolutely nothing productive. Celebrate the little wins like you just won an Oscar—minus the weepy speech.

And as a handy piece of advice: always have a backlog of content. This stash is your safety net for those days when motivation checks out without notice. Pre-preparing some posts or videos will save you from scrambling last-minute, maintaining your consistency even when you're lacking that magical spark. This is essentially your "bail you out of jail free card" in the Monopoly game of content creation.

Consistency and motivation are the dynamic duo that keeps your podcasting journey on track. They're the peanut butter and jelly of success—each great on their own, but together, they create something truly magical. So, keep showing up, keep creating, and keep that fire burning. Your audience (and your future self) will thank you for it.

Handling negative feedback and trolls So, you've poured your heart and soul into a podcast episode, and surprise, surprise, someone with the social skills of a honey badger leaves a nasty comment. Welcome to the internet! The first step in dealing with critics is to not take it personally. Remember, some folks just like to throw tomatoes from the peanut gallery.

If you want to preserve your peace of mind, start by evaluating the feedback. Is it constructive criticism or just a word salad of bitterness? If it's the former, take the gem of wisdom hidden in there and polish it. You might find that, amidst the bluster, there's a valid point that can help you improve your content.

For the unhelpful comments, practice your best Elsa impression and "Let It Go". Engaging with trolls can be like trying to teach algebra to a cat – frustrating and ultimately pointless. Besides, your energy is better spent creating awesome content than arguing with someone who probably has cheese puffs dust on their fingers.

Set up some ground rules for your community. A well-defined comment policy lets your audience know that while feedback is welcome, vitriol is not. For repeat offenders, the block button is your best friend. Don't hesitate to use it. You're in control here, not the trolls. Keep your digital space as you would your living room – clean, welcoming, and devoid of negativity.

One trick to keep your content environment positive is to amplify the good vibes. Encourage and highlight positive comments and messages. Give shout-outs to your biggest fans and those providing thoughtful feedback. This not only boosts morale for you but also fosters a supportive community atmosphere where trolls find it challenging to thrive.

It's essential for entrepreneurs, influencers, and creatives to remember that even Michelangelo had critics. It's part of the game. The world needs your voice, your perspective, and your creativity. Don't let the naysayers dim your shine. Keep hustling, keep creating, and let the haters watch your success from the sidelines.

And if all else fails, just remember: you can't please everyone. Even if you were a magical unicorn that pooped glitter and granted wishes, someone out there would still find a reason to complain. Focus on creating content that resonates with your target audience and aligns with your values. The right people will find you, appreciate you, and support you along the way.

Dealing with negative feedback and trolls is never fun, but it's an inevitable part of putting yourself out there. The key is to develop a thick skin, stay focused on your goals, and surround yourself with a supportive community that believes in your vision. And if you ever need a reminder of how awesome you are, just go back and read some of those glowing reviews and heartfelt messages from your loyal listeners. They're the ones who truly matter.

Reflection Questions:

1. What audio quality issues have you encountered in your podcasting journey, and how did you resolve them?
2. How can you create a sustainable podcasting schedule that keeps you consistent without leading to burnout?
3. What strategies can you implement to maintain a positive community and handle negative feedback constructively?

Congratulations, you've made it to the end of our podcasting adventure! By now, you should have a solid foundation for creating, launching, and growing your very own podcast. Remember, podcasting is a journey, not a destination. Keep learning, keep experimenting, and keep pushing yourself to create content that truly resonates with your audience.

Don't be afraid to make mistakes, try new things, and step outside your comfort zone. Some of the best moments in podcasting come from those unexpected detours and spontaneous bursts of creativity. Embrace the journey, and enjoy every step of the way.

And most importantly, never forget why you started this journey in the first place. Whether you're here to share your knowledge, inspire others, or simply have some fun, always stay true to your purpose and your passion. Your unique voice and perspective are what make your podcast truly special.

So, go forth and conquer the podcasting world, one episode at a time. We can't wait to hear all the amazing things you'll create!

Exercise:

� Develop a time management plan for balancing podcasting with your other commitments and responsibilities.

� Practice active listening and empathy skills for handling constructive feedback and criticism.

# Chapter 9: Growing Your Podcast Audience

Engaging with your listeners and building a community So, you've got a podcast, YouTube channel, or perhaps an Instagram account where you regularly go on about your love for artisanal cheese or the latest fintech trends. Now, how do you make sure people aren't just listening but are also falling head over heels in love with you and your content? Simple. You treat your audience like friends you haven't yet convinced to lend you a hundred bucks. You're not just broadcasting; you're engaging in a conversation. When someone comments on your post or sends you a message, respond like it's the last text from your crush. Be real, be humorous, and most importantly, be human. Slip in some emojis, laugh at your own jokes, or even share a meme or two. The most loyal followers are the ones who feel like they're part of your inside joke.

Now, let's talk about community-building. Creating a loyal following isn't some dark sorcery that requires moon phases and a Hogwarts letter. It's all about consistency and authenticity. Show up regularly, because no one wants to be ghosted in their own fandom. Be consistent in delivering quality content, but don't be afraid to share a bit of your personal journey. Your followers want to know you're human—one who perhaps spilled coffee on their laptop and lived to tell the tale. Engage with them through polls, Q&A sessions, or even live streams where they can see you, unedited and real. This personal touch makes them feel valued and included. Think of your community as a digital family where even crazy Uncle Bob is welcome.

Here's the secret sauce: collaboration. Joining forces with other creators or influencers not only amplifies your reach but also brings a new flavor to your audience. Think of it as cross-pollination—like when Batman joined forces with Superman. And if Batman can do it, so can you! Just make sure to choose collaborators who resonate with your values and style. This way, your combined audience feels like they're getting double the awesomeness without the whiplash from a sudden genre shift. Remember, building a community takes time and effort, just like building that IKEA bookshelf that's still missing a crucial screw. But stick to it, and you'll create a space where your audience feels not just like spectators but like they truly belong.

Building a community around your podcast is like tending to a garden. It requires constant nurturing, attention, and a whole lot of love. But when you see those first blooms of engagement, when you hear the excitement in your listeners' voices as they share their thoughts and experiences, it makes all the hard work worthwhile.

So, get out there and start cultivating those relationships. Respond to comments, share behind-the-scenes glimpses, and make your listeners feel like they're an integral part of your podcasting journey. Because in the end, that's what it's all about – creating a space where people feel heard, valued, and connected.

Collaborating with other podcasters and influencers So, you're thinking about collaborating with other podcasters and influencers? Good choice. Imagine Batman without Robin, peanut butter without jelly, or a disco without a mirror ball — just doesn't pop, right? Sharing the spotlight can be a game-changer for your brand. First up, find your partner in crime. Not literally. Browse through the podcasts and influencer profiles that align with your niche. Whether you're an entrepreneur, influencer, or someone just looking for a creative outlet, there's a match out there. Picture this: two brains, twice the ideas, and a whirlwind of creative energy that's bound to produce content that'll make your audience do a happy dance.

When you partner with influencers, don't just think of it as expanding your reach; think of it as expanding your empire. Consider their audience as a treasure trove. You're not just borrowing their fans; you're making them your own. Like adding pineapple to pizza — some might be skeptical at first, but once they take a bite, they're hooked. The key is to pick influencers with a fan base that vibes with your brand. You've got your classic chocolate and vanilla combo; that's the kind of synergy you're aiming for. Collaborate on joint contests, Q&A sessions, or even co-host events. The goal here is to have your audiences mingle like they're at a really great party where everyone leaves with new friends.

Once you've found your potential collaborator, it's time to slide into their DMs or send a message that's sprinkled with charm and wit. Keep it straightforward and easy to understand. No need for a Shakespearean sonnet — a simple, "Hey, I love what you do! Let's create something epic together" will suffice. Share your vision, outline the benefits, and voila, you're in. Now, the real magic starts — brainstorming sessions. Get ready for a roller coaster ride of ideas. Just remember, Rome wasn't built in a day and neither is a stellar collaboration. Take your time to plan it out and make it spontaneous yet organized.

When it comes to collaborations, don't be afraid to think outside the box. Sure, a joint podcast episode is a classic move, but why stop there? Consider creating a mini-series together, hosting a live event (virtual or in-person), or even launching a limited-edition product that ties into both your brands. The possibilities are endless!

And remember, collaboration isn't just about the end product – it's about the journey. Take the time to really get to know your collaborator, learn from their experiences, and have fun along the way. Some of the best collaborations are born from genuine friendships and a shared passion for creating awesome content.

Utilizing SEO and other strategies for discoverability Let's cut to the chase. SEO sounds fancy, but often feels like a riddle wrapped in an enigma. In simpler terms, it's about making sure Google can find your podcast faster than you can find a pair of matching socks. Imagine your podcast is a needle, and the internet is a haystack. Your job is to make that needle as shiny and magnetic as possible. Start with keywords - those magic words people type into the search bar. Play detective and figure out what keywords relate to your podcast topic. Use these words in your episode titles, descriptions, and even show notes. Sprinkle them around thoughtfully but don't go overboard. Think of it like seasoning a steak - sufficient to bring out flavors but not so much that it looks like it's straight off a salt flat. And don't overlook meta tags. They might sound techy and boring, but they're like the window display of a shop. These tidbits that appear in search results can significantly impact whether someone clicks to listen or scrolls on by.

All the SEO in the world won't help if no one's talking about your podcast. Time to employ some guerrilla marketing tactics. First up, be a guest on other podcasts. It's like crashing someone else's wedding and leaving with all the leftover cake. It gets your voice out there and introduces you to a whole new audience. Also, find creative ways to engage on social media. No, not another boring "New Episode Alert!" post. Share behind-the-scenes glimpses, funny mishaps during recordings, or the incredulous sound of your co-host realizing they've been talking into a muted mic. Instagram Reels, TikTok videos, Twitter threads - these can be gold mines for snagging attention. And don't forget to encourage listener reviews. Positive reviews are like Yelp for fine dining - they invite new listeners to come in and sit down for a meal. Prompt listeners to leave reviews with a gentle nudge, maybe even sweeten the pot with a small giveaway or a fun on-air shoutout.

Finally, remember collaboration is your secret weapon. Team up with influencers or other podcasters. Host a joint episode or find a way to cross-promote. The goal is to create a ripple effect, where the reach of their audience overlaps with yours, causing a delightful wave of new listeners heading your way. Think of it as getting a VIP pass into an already crowded party. And who doesn't love a good party?

SEO and discoverability might seem like daunting tasks, but with a little creativity and a lot of hustle, you can make your podcast stand out in a crowded digital landscape. Remember, it's not about gaming the system or employing sneaky tactics – it's about making sure your target audience can find you and fall in love with your content.

So, roll up your sleeves, put on your detective hat, and start unraveling the mysteries of SEO. Experiment with different strategies, track your results, and don't be afraid to adjust your approach as you go. And most importantly, never lose sight of why you started your podcast in the first place – to share your unique voice and perspective with the world.

With a solid SEO strategy, a dash of guerrilla marketing, and a sprinkle of collaboration magic, you'll be well on your way to attracting a loyal and engaged audience that can't wait to hear what you have to say next.

Reflection Questions:

1. What strategies can you implement to foster a sense of community among your podcast listeners?
2. Who are some potential collaborators in your niche, and how can you approach them for a partnership?
3. What keywords and phrases are most relevant to your podcast, and how can you integrate them into your content and metadata?

Congratulations, you've made it to the end of our podcasting journey! By now, you should have a solid foundation for creating, launching, and growing your very own podcast. But remember, the learning doesn't stop here. The world of podcasting is constantly evolving, with new trends, technologies, and strategies emerging all the time.

To stay ahead of the curve, make a commitment to continuous learning and improvement. Attend podcasting conferences, join online communities, and never stop experimenting with new ideas and approaches. And don't be afraid to lean on your fellow podcasters for support and guidance – after all, we're all in this together!

As you embark on this exciting new chapter in your creative journey, always remember the power of your unique voice and perspective. Your podcast has the potential to inspire, educate, and entertain people from all walks of life, and that's a pretty incredible thing.

So, go forth and podcast your heart out! We can't wait to see (and hear) all the amazing things you'll create. Happy podcasting!

Exercise:

� Identify 3 potential guests or collaborators in your niche and reach out to them for a potential interview or partnership.

� Create a social media content calendar for promoting your podcast and engaging with your audience.

# Chapter 10: Keeping Your Podcast Fresh and Exciting

Brainstorming new topics and episode ideas Alright, let's dive into the meaty bits right away. Idea generation is like doing mental gymnastics while juggling flaming swords - fun, sweaty, and potentially hazardous if you overdo it. Let's get straight into some snazzy yet straightforward tactics to keep those creative juices flowing without singeing your eyebrows off. Entrepreneurs and influencers: think of your brain as a gold mine. Just because you've hit a vein of rich content ideas doesn't mean you stop digging. Sometimes the best ideas are lurking just beneath the surface.

First, relax; yes, you heard that right. Counterintuitive as it may seem, brilliant ideas often strike when you're not actively searching for them. Take a walk, do some yoga (yes, even if you can't touch your toes), or engage in a completely unrelated activity like baking cookies. Inspiration might hit you in the midst of a dough-making epiphany. For those constantly on the go, voice memo apps are a lifesaver. Mutters of genius content deserve more than a forgotten post-it note.

For the trend chasers among us, keep your eyes glued to social media and news outlets. Tools like Google Trends, Twitter hashtags, and Reddit threads are like crystal balls that show you what's sizzling hot right now. Jumping on a trending topic is like surfing a massive wave - thrilling, with the potential to sweep you a long way if timed just right.

And because we don't discriminate, whether you're a woman, man, or unicorn looking for your own creative outlet, crowdsource ideas. No, this doesn't mean standing on your desk and shouting at your coworkers (though that could be fun). Ask your audience what they want to hear about. Hold polls, Q&A sessions, or even comment dives to pick up on recurring themes. Your best ideas might just be hiding in plain sight, waiting for you to ask the right question.

So, to keep that idea machine well-oiled and running smoothly, balance relaxation with active research and audience engagement. And remember, the look of sheer genius in your eyes as you jot down the next big idea will be worth the occasional weird stare from passersby. Keep a notebook handy - or if you're into gadgets, your note-taking app - because the next big topic might pop into your head when you least expect it.

Another gold mine for topic ideas? Your own life experiences! As an entrepreneur, influencer, or creative soul, you've undoubtedly had your fair share of triumphs, failures, and everything in between. Don't be afraid to get personal and share those stories with your audience. They'll appreciate the authenticity and relatability, and you might just inspire someone who's going through a similar situation.

And let's not forget about the power of collaboration. Reach out to other experts in your field, or even in completely different industries, and see if they'd be interested in joining you for an episode. Not only will you gain fresh insights and perspectives, but you'll also tap into their audience, potentially expanding your reach.

Remember, brainstorming is a muscle – the more you flex it, the stronger it becomes. Make idea generation a regular part of your creative process, and soon enough, you'll have more topics than you know what to do with. And that's a pretty great problem to have!

Experimenting with different formats and styles Let's dive headfirst into the joy of trying out new styles and formats. Imagine your content is like a wardrobe. Sometimes you want to rock a business suit, other times you might reach for that wild Hawaiian shirt. Entrepreneurs out there, spice up those boring business updates with a narrative style. Tell a story about that time your project almost went belly up and how you saved it last minute. It's way more engaging than a dry project report. Influencers, toss in a quiz or poll in your next post. Nothing screams "I'm fun and interesting" like interactive content. Not only does it keep your followers on their toes, but it also gives you insights into their preferences. Win-win!

Style shifts are like plot twists in a novel—they keep your audience guessing and coming back for more. Men and women alike, let's shake things up. Write that next blog in a dialect or pretend it's a conversation between two old friends. People love relatable content, and nothing says "relatable" like a casual chat. For those seeking a creative outlet, play around with different color schemes and fonts in your emails or marketing materials. You'd be surprised how much a slight change in visual style can make your content pop and feel fresh.

Here's a hot tip: combine formats for that ultimate wow factor. Start with a punchy blog post, then switch to a video or infographic to dive deeper. This mix will keep your audience glued to your content from start to finish. Preparing for a big presentation? How about turning your bullet points into a comic strip? It's memorable, and let's face it, who can resist a good laugh in the middle of a soul-crushing quarterly review?

When it comes to your podcast, don't be afraid to switch up your episode formats from time to time. If you typically do solo monologues, try bringing in a co-host or guest for a lively discussion. If you're usually all about the interviews, consider doing a deep-dive solo episode on a topic you're passionate about.

And hey, why not take your podcast out of the studio and into the wild? Record an episode at a relevant event, conference, or even just at your favorite coffee shop. The change of scenery can breathe new life into your content and give your listeners a fresh perspective.

The key is to keep your audience on their toes while still staying true to your brand and message. Experimenting with different formats and styles shows that you're not afraid to take risks and keep things interesting. Plus, it gives you a chance to flex your creative muscles and discover new ways to connect with your listeners.

So, go ahead – mix it up, try something new, and have fun with it! Your audience will appreciate the variety, and you might just discover a new format or style that takes your podcast to the next level.

Evolving with your audience and staying relevant First things first: if you think staying social means just posting pictures of your breakfast burrito on Instagram, think again. Staying social means listening to your listeners. Your audience is like a curious cat—they've got questions, comments, and sometimes, claws. Hear them out! Respond to their comments, ask them what they want to see more of, and maybe sprinkle in some cat memes. The secret sauce here is to make them feel like they're part of your journey, not just spectators in a digital coliseum.

Now, let's talk content. Your content should evolve as you and your audience grow. Think of it like a potluck dinner. One day, everyone's in the mood for tacos; the next, it's all about sushi. Don't be the person who only brings potato salad to every event. Diversify! Maybe you started out focusing on email marketing but noticed your followers are gravitating toward social media strategies. Pivot with pizzazz! Provide content that addresses their current interests and challenges, but make sure it aligns with your niche. You can even repurpose older content with a fresh spin to keep the party going.

Here's a golden nugget you can actually use: schedule regular "check-ins" with your audience. Ask them what they love, what they hate, and what they can't live without. You'll get unfiltered opinions, and sometimes a roasting. But this is gold! Use these insights to tweak your strategies and deliver exactly what they're craving. Remember, relevancy isn't a sprint; it's a marathon with a lot of caffeine breaks. Keep the conversation flowing, stay updated with trends, and most importantly, remember to have fun! If you're not enjoying yourself, it'll show—and who wants to follow a grumpy guru?

Evolving with your audience also means being open to change and willing to adapt. Maybe you started your podcast with a specific target audience in mind, but over time, you've noticed a shift in your listener demographics. Don't be afraid to adjust your content and messaging to better serve your new audience.

And remember, staying relevant doesn't mean jumping on every trending bandwagon or chasing after the latest shiny object. It means staying true to your core values and message while finding ways to connect with your audience's changing needs and interests.

One way to do this is by regularly seeking feedback from your listeners. Encourage them to leave reviews, send in questions or topic suggestions, and engage with you on social media. Use this feedback to inform your content strategy and ensure that you're always providing value to your audience.

Another way to stay relevant is by collaborating with other podcasters or influencers who share your values and target audience. By cross-promoting each other's content and appearing on each other's shows, you can introduce your podcast to new listeners and keep things fresh and exciting for your existing audience.

At the end of the day, evolving with your audience and staying relevant is all about building genuine relationships and providing consistent value. So, keep those lines of communication open, stay curious and adaptable, and never stop striving to create content that resonates with your listeners.

Reflection Questions:

1. What are some unconventional ways you can brainstorm new topic ideas for your podcast?
2. Which new format or style are you most excited to experiment with in your upcoming episodes?
3. How can you incorporate regular audience feedback and engagement into your podcast strategy to ensure you're evolving with your listeners?

And there you have it, folks – the ultimate guide to keeping your podcast fresh, engaging, and relevant in an ever-changing digital landscape. Remember, the key to podcasting success is to stay curious, stay creative, and never stop pushing yourself to try new things.

Sure, it might feel scary to step outside your comfort zone and experiment with new formats or styles, but that's where the magic happens. That's where you'll find new ways to connect with your audience, express your unique voice, and build a podcast that truly stands out from the crowd.

So, keep brainstorming those big ideas, keep experimenting with different approaches, and keep evolving alongside your listeners. And most importantly, keep having fun! Because at the end of the day, that's what podcasting is all about – sharing your passion, your knowledge, and your creativity with the world in a way that feels authentic and enjoyable to you.

We can't wait to see where your podcasting journey takes you next. Happy podcasting!

Exercise:

◈ Challenge yourself to experiment with a new episode format or style, such as an interview, co-hosted episode, or solo rant.

◈ Survey your audience to gather feedback and ideas for future episode topics and guests.

# Chapter 11: Leveraging Your Podcast for Personal Branding

Integrating your podcast with your overall brand So, you've decided to jump on the podcast train – welcome aboard! But don't just slap your logo on a podcast cover and call it a day. The real fun begins when you make your podcast an extension of your brand's voice. Think of it like introducing a new family member at a reunion; they need to fit right in with the rest or there's gonna be some awkward dinner conversations. Your podcast should reflect your brand's values, tone, and even its quirks. If your brand is all about high energy and humor, your podcast should make people laugh (or at least snort) within the first five minutes. Use your brand's color scheme on your podcast cover art, include your tagline, and have your hosts mention your brand mission in their intros. It's like giving your audience a delicious baby carrot before they get to munch on the main course.

Ever notice how you'll recognize your favorite show within the first ten seconds? That's consistency, baby. Make sure your podcast episodes align with your overall brand message and marketing campaigns. This isn't the time to go rogue and talk about your cat's dietary preferences (unless you're running a pet store, then go wild). If your brand is all about eco-friendly living, make sure your episodes revolve around sustainability tips, interviews with green living experts, and eco-friendly product reviews. Your listeners should never have that awkward "Wait, what?" moment – keep them nodding along, feeling like they're in the right place. Your brand voice should be the same across all platforms, whether it's on your blog, social media, or your sassy podcast offering. Trust us, your audience will appreciate the seamless experience and trust your brand even more. Consistency is key, like showing up to every family gathering and always remembering Aunt Vicky's birthday.

Never underestimate the power of cross-promotion. Mention your other brand assets during your podcast. Got a killer email newsletter? Plug it in. Just wrote a blog post that's hotter than a stolen tamale? Drop that link like it's hot! Direct your podcast listeners to your website, social media profiles, and any other touchpoints where they can engage with your brand. This positions your podcast as one piece of the bigger puzzle and helps reinforce your brand's presence in their lives. You're essentially weaving a big, warm, branded blanket that keeps wrapping itself around your audience until they're snugly loyal. And hey, making your podcast part of your overall brand strategy isn't rocket science – it's about creating a coherent and recognizable experience. So go ahead, knit that blanket with gusto, and watch your brand presence reach new cozy heights.

Another way to seamlessly integrate your podcast with your brand is by featuring your own products or services in your episodes. But wait, before you start shouting "BUY MY STUFF!" into the mic, let's talk about how to do this without sounding like a late-night infomercial. The key is to provide value first and foremost. If you're discussing a problem your target audience faces, mention how your product or service can help solve that problem. Share case studies or success stories from customers who have benefited from what you offer. And always, always, always prioritize educating and entertaining your listeners over making a hard sell.

Remember, your podcast is a powerful tool for building trust and establishing your brand as an authority in your niche. By consistently delivering high-quality content that aligns with your brand values and message, you'll create a loyal fanbase that not only tunes in week after week but also becomes your biggest advocates and customers.

So, go forth and create that podcast magic! Weave it into the tapestry of your brand, and watch as your audience falls in love with not just your voice, but your entire brand experience.

Networking and making connections through your podcast So you want to be a Network Ninja, huh? Think of yourself as a social martial artist, swiftly kicking your way into hearts and inboxes everywhere. The good news is, your podcast is your dojo. First thing's first: let's talk about leveraging this audio playground to build relationships. Imagine your podcast as a giant, cozy coffee shop where you get to invite anyone you want for a chat, and guess what? They almost always say yes! It's like offering someone a golden ticket to share their story, flex their expertise, and boost their brand. Who wouldn't want that?

Here's a ninja move for you: focus on quality over quantity. Instead of trying to be everyone's BFF (which is exhausting, trust me), hone in on a few key players in your industry. Slide into their DMs, but make sure you're not coming off like a desperate ninja in training. Do some research, reference their work, and make that first contact count. When you invite them to your podcast, make them see the mutual benefits – it's a win-win. They get exposure and a platform, you get killer content and a connection. Everybody high-kicks with joy.

Connection creation is your next secret weapon. Leverage your platform to create opportunities not just for yourself, but for your guests as well. Promote them fiercely. Make them feel like rockstars – because they are! Tag them in your social media posts, send out email blasts, sprinkle their name around like glitter. Offer to write them a glowing LinkedIn recommendation. Create a little fanfare. By doing this, you're building bridges that lead to amazing opportunities, like speaking gigs, partnerships, or even friendships (yes, those still exist in the business world).

But hold up – don't forget to follow up. After the mic turns off, the real relationship-building begins. Send a thank-you note, maybe a small gift, or even just a heartfelt email. Keep the conversation going. Share their upcoming work with your audience, and periodically check in. You're not just a one-and-done ninja; you're in this for the long game. Keep the communication lines open so you're top of mind when they think of collaborative opportunities.

Finally, keep sharpening your ninja skills. Always be learning, adapting, and growing your podcast. Take feedback from your listeners and your guests. This is your dojo, and the more skilled you are, the more appealing you become as someone who isn't just there to take, but also to give. So, gear up, ninja – your podcast is your ticket to becoming a networking sensei.

And remember, networking is a two-way street. As much as you want to leverage your podcast to build relationships and create opportunities for yourself, make sure you're also giving back to your guests and your community. Share your own insights, experiences, and connections. Be a resource and a supporter for others in your industry. The more you give, the more you'll receive in return.

Networking through your podcast isn't just about expanding your professional circle; it's about building genuine, mutually beneficial relationships. It's about creating a community of like-minded individuals who support, inspire, and elevate each other. And by consistently showing up, providing value, and being a giver, you'll become the kind of person everyone wants to know, collaborate with, and recommend.

So, put on your networking ninja gear, fire up that mic, and start building those connections. Your podcast is your secret weapon, and the world is waiting for you to make your move.

Using your podcast as a platform for your expertise and passions Let's face it, you're basically the Einstein of your field, except you don't have to battle with that wild hairdo (or maybe you do; no judgment here). Why keep all that brainpower to yourself when the world is out there starving for your genius? That's where a podcast comes in handy. Imagine explaining quantum physics to your cat—it's the same excitement, but your listeners won't wander off to nap halfway through. Whether you're an entrepreneur with a knack for spotting trends or an influencer who knows which avocado toast gets the most likes, your expertise needs the limelight. Start each episode with a nugget of wisdom wrapped in your unique style, and soon, people will be quoting you more than their motivational fridge magnets.

Now, let's talk passion. Not the romantic kind, unless your passion involves matchmaking algorithms that also bake perfect soufflés. We're talking about the stuff that makes you jump out of bed faster than when you realize you're out of coffee. If you're an enthusiast of any kind—from knitting cat sweaters to performing Shakespeare in Klingon—your podcast is your stage. Sharing your passions with the world isn't just about getting validation (though, yes, it feels amazing); it's about finding fellow oddballs who vibe with your enthusiasm. So, turn on that mic and geek out, because your tribe is out there, probably also in pajamas, waiting.

When it comes to using your podcast to showcase expertise and passion, blend them like a smoothie—equal parts knowledge and zeal, with a sprinkle of humor for taste. Let's say you're a financial advisor who also happens to love improv comedy. Why not teach budgeting techniques using hilarious scenarios, like saving money for a llama farm? Or if you're a fitness guru with a penchant for sci-fi, discuss workout routines fit for surviving an alien invasion. Keeping things light and fun not only makes your podcast approachable but also memorable. Listeners are more likely to return when they're learning and laughing.

But wait, there's more! Your podcast isn't just a platform for sharing your expertise and passions; it's also a powerful tool for establishing yourself as a thought leader in your industry. By consistently delivering valuable insights, fresh perspectives, and actionable advice, you'll build trust with your audience and position yourself as the go-to expert in your field.

And as you share your knowledge and enthusiasm, don't forget to be vulnerable and authentic. Share your failures along with your successes, your doubts along with your certainties. This vulnerability creates a deeper connection with your listeners and makes you more relatable and likable. After all, people don't just want to learn from experts; they want to learn from real human beings who have been where they are and have faced similar challenges.

Finally, use your podcast to inspire and empower your listeners. Share stories of how you've overcome obstacles, pursued your dreams, and made a difference in your industry or community. Encourage your audience to take action, chase their own passions, and make their mark on the world. When you use your platform to uplift and motivate others, you'll create a loyal fanbase that not only respects your expertise but also admires your character and values.

So, whether you're a marketing maven, a coding wizard, or a crochet connoisseur, let your podcast be the megaphone for your expertise and passions. Share your knowledge, your enthusiasm, and your authentic self with the world, and watch as your personal brand soars to new heights.

Reflection Questions:

1. How can you ensure that your podcast aligns with and reinforces your overall brand message and values?
2. What are some specific ways you can leverage your podcast to build relationships and create networking opportunities?
3. How can you balance sharing your expertise and passions with being vulnerable and relatable to your audience?

And there you have it, folks – the ultimate guide to leveraging your podcast for personal branding success. By integrating your podcast with your overall brand, networking like a ninja, and using your platform to showcase your expertise and passions, you'll be well on your way to building a powerful personal brand that opens doors and creates endless opportunities.

But remember, personal branding through your podcast isn't just about promoting yourself; it's about serving your audience, providing value, and making a positive impact in your industry and beyond. It's about being authentic, vulnerable, and relatable while also establishing yourself as a trusted authority and thought leader.

So, as you continue on your podcasting journey, keep these strategies in mind and always stay true to yourself and your mission. Don't be afraid to experiment, take risks, and try new things. The beauty of podcasting is that it allows you to constantly evolve, grow, and reinvent yourself and your brand.

And most importantly, have fun with it! Your passion, enthusiasm, and joy will shine through in every episode and will be the secret ingredient that keeps your audience coming back for more.

So, go forth and conquer the podcasting world, one episode at a time. Your personal brand (and your adoring fans) will thank you for it!

Exercise:

◈ Update your social media profiles and website to include your podcast and position yourself as an expert in your niche.

◈ Create a media kit or one-sheet for your podcast to share with potential sponsors, guests, or media outlets.

# Chapter 12: Building a Supportive Podcasting Community

Finding mentors and peer support If you think finding a mentor is like searching for a needle in a haystack, let me tell you it's more like searching for Wi-Fi at a campsite. It's out there, you just need the right hunting skills. Let's demystify this. Mentors are the magical unicorns of your entrepreneurial journey but, unlike unicorns, they actually exist. They're just busy being successful, but they'd make time for an aspiring you. Think of it as celebrity spotting, but with valuable life lessons attached.

First, you need to adopt the omnipresent social media stalker role, minus the creepy vibes. LinkedIn is your go-to platform. Stalk (ahem, research) leaders in your industry, attend their webinars, comment on their posts—basically make it known you exist. But don't spam their inboxes with "Can you be my mentor?" That's like proposing marriage on the first date. Build a connection by showing genuine interest in their work.

Once you've flagged their radar, slide into their DMs with a respectful message outlining your admiration for their journey and how you'd love a pinch of their wisdom. Don't be generic. Make it clear you know them and their work. Remember, they're more likely to accept if you're specific about what you hope to gain from the mentorship, not just "teach me everything."

Mentorship secured? Great, let's move on to enlisting the Avengers—your peer group. Peer support is crucial because misery and triumph both love company. Your peers are the ones who'll understand your entrepreneurial woes at a level your family never will. They know the pain of cue-less podcast listeners and blog posts read by your dog and three loyal friends.

Look for peer groups on forums like Reddit or Facebook Groups. Attend meetups—in person or virtual—and stop hanging out in the same digital spots as your audience. Instead, frequent the places where creators go to vent, learn, and grow. Engaging with a community of like-minded individuals is akin to having a mirror that not only shows your current self but also reflects a dozen possible better selves.

Zero in on a few dedicated souls who are in a similar stage as you. Make a WhatsApp group or set a regular Zoom meeting. This is your entrepreneurial bromance or womance forming! Share your wins, dissect your fails, and exchange tips—like which breath mints keep your voice crisp for those late-night recording marathons.

A great trick to keep the momentum is to find an accountability buddy. This is the friend who will ping you if you missed your daily goal of creating content and will virtually high-five you when you hit a milestone. They not only hold your feet to the fire but also bring the marshmallows. Your peer group is your safety net and motivational squad rolled into one.

To wrap it up with a practical tip: Always take initiative. Don't wait for a magical invite to the "I help you, you help me" club. Reach out, find your tribe, and soon you'll cultivate the right blend of mentors and peers who're ready to elevate your game, creatively and entrepreneurially.

And remember, mentorship and peer support aren't just about receiving guidance and encouragement; they're also about giving back. As you grow and evolve in your podcasting journey, make sure to pay it forward by offering your own insights, experiences, and support to those who are just starting out. Share your successes, your failures, and your lessons learned. Be the mentor and the peer that you wish you had when you were first starting out.

Building a supportive podcasting community isn't just about advancing your own career; it's about contributing to the growth and success of the entire industry. It's about fostering a culture of collaboration, generosity, and mutual respect. And when you approach mentorship and peer support with this mindset, you'll find that the rewards extend far beyond your own personal achievements.

So, don't be afraid to reach out, connect, and build those relationships. Embrace the power of community, and watch as your podcasting journey takes flight in ways you never could have imagined.

Attending podcasting conferences and events Ever felt like a hermit stuck in a Wi-Fi cave? Well, it's time to dust off that socially acceptable attire and put on your networking hat. Conferences and events in the podcasting world are like a funhouse mirror—except instead of distorting your image, they reflect an amplified version of your potential. Here, networking is less about boring handshakes and more about juicy conversations that could spark your next big idea. Whether you're an entrepreneur ready to pitch a podcast empire, an influencer looking to boost your brand, or simply someone eager to dive into a creative outlet, these events are your playground. Grab some business cards (yes, they still exist) and practice your elevator pitch; you never know who might be your next collaborator or sponsor.

If you're thinking conferences are just for the corporate world, think again. These gatherings are packed with sessions that aim to strip away the mystique of podcasting. Imagine roundtable discussions where jargon translates into everyday speak, and workshops that turn bewildering tech stuff into child's play. It's like meeting old friends—if your old friends were experts in leveraging RSS feeds and mastering monetization strategies. The cherry on the top? The keynotes by industry titans are gold mines of inspiration. Take notes, but more importantly, ask questions. Here's the kicker: the more dumb you think your question is, the more minds it will enlighten.

Time to talk about the nitty-gritty, because let's face it, we're all scavengers for free stuff. Beyond the swag bags that make you feel like a superstar, there's an array of tools and services that can elevate your podcasting game from amateur hour to prime time. Stop by the exhibitors' booths not just to snag freebies, but to discover the latest gizmos and gadgets that simplify production or revolutionize editing. And don't worry if you geek out visibly; everyone else is too. Consider this: one demo could save you hours of trial and error back home. Besides, swapping stories with vendors might just land you a discount or an insider tip.

Ready for a nugget of wisdom? Start by setting clear objectives before you even register for the event. Want to find a co-host, secure advertisers, or learn advanced techniques? Identifying your goals keeps you from wandering aimlessly amidst the sea of podcasters. Connect in advance via social media, and don't hesitate to reach out to speakers or participants you'd like to meet. Conferences can feel overwhelming, but remember: everyone here is in the same boat, rowing towards creative fulfillment. Enjoy the ride, and don't forget to follow up with new acquaintances post-event. A simple "great meeting you" email can transform fleeting encounters into lasting connections.

But attending conferences and events isn't just about what you can gain; it's also about what you can contribute. Look for opportunities to share your own knowledge and experiences, whether it's through speaking on a panel, leading a workshop, or simply engaging in meaningful conversations with fellow attendees. By giving back to the community, you'll not only establish yourself as a valuable resource and thought leader, but you'll also foster a sense of camaraderie and mutual support that extends beyond the event itself.

And don't forget to have fun! Podcasting conferences and events are a celebration of creativity, innovation, and passion. Embrace the energy, the excitement, and the sheer joy of being surrounded by people who share your love for this incredible medium. Strike up conversations, make new friends, and let yourself be inspired by the stories and experiences of those around you.

Attending podcasting conferences and events can be a game-changer for your personal and professional growth. So, mark your calendar, pack your bags, and get ready to immerse yourself in the vibrant, dynamic world of podcasting. Your next big breakthrough might just be one conference away!

Seeking feedback and collaboration with fellow podcasters Alright, you're a podcasting maestro, but even Mozart had a mentor. Seeking feedback is essential, not because you're off-key, but because even stars need spotlight adjustments. Approach feedback like it's your morning coffee – essential, invigorating, and sometimes a little bitter. Reach out to your listeners, your loyal audience, because who better to tell you what works than the people who tune in every week? Use social media polls, email newsletters, and comments to collect their thoughts. And don't be shy – ask them outright, "What's hitting the right notes, and where are we falling flat?"

Now, let's dive into this collaboration pool, and don't worry, the water's fine. Working with fellow podcasters is like assembling an Avengers team, but instead of battling Thanos, you're battling obscurity. Find podcasters in your niche, or even better, in slightly different niches – think chocolate meeting peanut butter. The crossover appeal is real, folks. Hop on their show, invite them to yours, banter, and make magic.

This cross-pollination doesn't just grow your audience; it introduces fresh ideas and perspectives.

Let's get real practical. Slide into their DMs – yes, I said it. A professionally casual message can work wonders. "Hey, love what you're doing! Fancy a collab?" goes a long way. Attend podcasting events, both virtual and in-person, and network like a butterfly on Red Bull. Get to know people, establish rapport, and before long, your podcasting family expands. Start small if need be; a brief guest segment or a shoutout can pave the way for bigger collaborations.

Finally, keep things spicy and fresh. Use new formats, try out live shows, or co-host specials. This not only keeps the audience engaged but also showcases your versatility. Remember, feedback and collaboration are your secret sauces. You don't just want to make a podcast; you want to create an experience that leaves your audience craving more. Keep experimenting, keep reaching out, and watch your empire grow.

But here's the thing about feedback and collaboration: it's not always easy to hear or implement. Sometimes, the feedback you receive might sting a little (or a lot), and the collaboration process might hit a few snags along the way. That's okay. It's all part of the growth process.

When you receive feedback, take a deep breath and approach it with an open mind. Remember, even the most critical feedback comes from a place of wanting to see you succeed. Take what resonates, leave what doesn't, and always express gratitude for the time and effort someone put into sharing their thoughts with you.

And when it comes to collaboration, communication is key. Be clear about your expectations, your boundaries, and your creative vision. Listen actively to your collaborator's ideas and concerns, and be willing to compromise and find solutions that work for everyone involved.

Collaboration is a two-way street, and the most successful partnerships are built on a foundation of mutual respect, trust, and open communication.

Seeking feedback and collaboration with fellow podcasters isn't just about improving your own show; it's about contributing to the growth and evolution of the entire podcasting community. By opening yourself up to constructive criticism and creative partnerships, you're not only elevating your own craft, but you're also helping to push the medium forward in exciting new directions.

So, put yourself out there. Seek feedback with an open heart and an eager mind. Collaborate with reckless abandon and infectious enthusiasm. Embrace the power of community, and watch as your podcast (and the podcasting world at large) soars to new heights.

Reflection Questions:

1. Who are some potential mentors or industry leaders you admire, and how can you start building relationships with them?
2. What are some podcasting communities or peer groups you can join to connect with like-minded creators and seek support?
3. Which podcasting conferences or events are you most excited to attend, and what specific goals do you hope to achieve by participating?

And there you have it, folks – the ultimate guide to building a supportive podcasting community. By finding mentors and peer support, attending conferences and events, and seeking feedback and collaboration with fellow podcasters, you'll be well on your way to creating a thriving network of creative allies and industry advocates.

But remember, building a community isn't just about what you can gain; it's about what you can give. It's about showing up, contributing your unique voice and perspective, and supporting others on their own podcasting journeys. It's about fostering a culture of generosity, empathy, and mutual growth.

So, as you navigate the exciting world of podcasting, always keep the power of community at the forefront of your mind. Reach out to others, offer your support and expertise, and be open to receiving the same in return. Celebrate your fellow podcasters' successes, learn from their challenges, and always remember that you're part of something bigger than yourself.

And most importantly, have fun with it! Building a supportive podcasting community should be a joyful, enriching experience – one that fills you with a sense of purpose, belonging, and endless possibility. So, embrace the journey, cherish the connections, and never stop believing in the transformative power of your voice and your story.

The podcasting world is waiting for you. Go out there and make some magic!

Exercise:

⍰ Join 2-3 online podcasting communities or forums and introduce yourself and your podcast.

⍰ Attend a local podcasting meetup or event and practice your networking and elevator pitch skills.

# Chapter 13: Balancing Podcasting with Other Commitments

Managing your time and energy effectively Picture this: you're diligently working on your latest entrepreneurial venture, trying to be the next Mark Zuckerberg or Oprah, but instead of making waves, you're swimming in an endless ocean of sticky notes and calendar alerts. Time management can feel like taming a herd of wild squirrels hyped up on energy drinks. The key to juggling all your pods and personal aspirations without spontaneously combusting lies in a few nifty tricks. First off, let's talk multitasking. Spoiler alert: it's not real. Our brains are not designed to write emails while simultaneously planning world domination and doodling future tattoo ideas. Instead, try time blocking. Dedicate chunks of time to specific tasks and stick to them as if you're attached with industrial-strength Velcro. Now, for project pods – think of these as mini-projects within your greater goals. Break your workload into bite-sized, manageable pods and tackle them one at a time. It's like eating a large pizza slice by slice rather than trying to unhinge your jaw.

Maintaining your energy is like being the manager of the world's hardest-working battery – yourself. Entrepreneurs, influencers, and creative souls often run on the fumes of passion, caffeine, and sheer willpower. But eventually, even the most passionate generator will sputter to a halt without proper care. Let's start with the basics: food, sleep, and hydration. Yes, you do need to consume things other than triple-espresso shots and protein bars. Your body is a temple; treat it more like the Taj Mahal than a dehydrated, crumbling ruin. Regular meals, a respectable number of hours in dreamland, and copious amounts of water could transform you from a stressed mess into a zesty powerhouse. For those on-the-go moments, keep energy snacks handy – nuts, fruits, maybe a cheeky granola bar. And don't forget the most underrated energy booster: laughter. Surround yourself with people who make you laugh, watch silly videos online, or even practice your own stand-up routine – humor is a great way to recharge.

To balance your time and energy seamlessly, there's a secret weapon. Drumroll, please: it's the art of saying no. Every task, project, or coffee meet-up with a long-lost acquaintance you agree to takes a bite out of your finite allotment of time and energy. Prioritizing isn't selfish; it's essential. Being clear about your primary goals allows you to filter out distractions like an Instagram feed filters out low-quality selfies. Speaking of social media, let's address the influencer in you. Schedule your posts, responses, and audience engagement instead of treating your notifications like a game of Whac-A-Mole. This not only saves time but preserves your sanity. Boundaries are your best friend; protect them fiercely.

And here's a nugget of wisdom that's often overlooked: take breaks. Yes, you heard that right. Step away from your desk, your phone, and your never-ending to-do list. Take a walk, do some stretches, or just stare out the window and let your mind wander. These mini-breaks are like hitting the reset button on your brain, allowing you to come back to your tasks with renewed focus and creativity.

Remember, effective time and energy management isn't about working harder; it's about working smarter. It's about being intentional with your resources, prioritizing what matters most, and giving yourself permission to rest and recharge when needed. And when you master this delicate balance, you'll find that you're not just more productive, but also more fulfilled and joyful in both your podcasting pursuits and your personal life.

So, grab your calendar, your energy snacks, and your boundary-setting hat, and get ready to take control of your time and energy like the boss you are. Your podcast (and your sanity) will thank you for it.

Setting boundaries and avoiding burnout Let's dive straight into the Boundary Basics: there's a universal truth rarely discussed at dinner parties or business meetings – your time is your most precious commodity. Ever had that moment when you're knee-deep in a project and a quick question from a colleague spirals into a full-blown brainstorming session about whether pineapple belongs on pizza or not? Next thing you know, an hour has evaporated, and you've achieved nothing but a slightly stronger opinion about exotic pizza toppings. Entrepreneurs, influencers, and all creative souls must guard their schedule like it's the last slice at a pizza party. Create office hours, even if your office is the sofa in your living room. Allocate specific times for deep work and strategy, and let everyone know – politely but firmly – that you're unavailable then. Be ruthless with time-blocking. If WFH life has blurred the lines, slap those boundaries back into place, pronto.

Now, let's flip the switch to Burnout Busters. You've seen it before – the frazzled influencer who promises to provide life-changing content but instead shares a twelve-part series on different kinds of bread (hey, love carbs, but come on). Here's the hard truth: if you constantly burn the midnight oil, you'll soon be left with nothing but soot. Passion projects can turn into draining endeavors if you don't learn the art of stepping back. Literally. Step away from your workspace periodically. Schedule "you time" like it's a crucial meeting with the CEO of your life because, well, it is. Engage in activities that recharge you. Reading a non-business book, binge-watching guilty pleasures, or even the sacred afternoon nap – it's all fair game. Sleep, eat well, and hydrate like you're in a cheesy sports movie montage, gearing up for the big game. You'll thank yourself later when you're not reduced to a caffeine-dependent zombie.

To sum up these chapters without saying "to sum up," remember this: your passion and creativity thrive on balance. Protecting your time isn't selfish; it's essential. And maintaining your spark with burnout-busting rituals will keep you not just in the game, but winning at it. So, block out distractions and nourish your mind and body with the care they deserve. The next big idea or joyous creation is already brewing – just make sure you're fit and ready for it. Also, always know when to switch off your business brain mode and let yourself daydream – that's where the magic truly happens. As a practical tip, try using your 'out of office' autoresponder to schedule mini-vacations for yourself – even if it's just to delve into that bread documentary. Because, life's too short to be anything but passionate and joyful.

And here's the kicker: setting boundaries and avoiding burnout isn't just about preserving your own well-being; it's also about protecting the quality of your work and the integrity of your relationships. When you're overworked, stressed, and spread too thin, the quality of your podcast (and everything else in your life) suffers. You're not able to show up as your best self, and that's a disservice to both you and your audience.

So, make a commitment to yourself and your craft: set those boundaries, prioritize self-care, and create a sustainable podcasting practice that allows you to thrive both on and off the mic. Your listeners will feel the difference, and your passion for podcasting will remain a source of joy and fulfillment, rather than a one-way ticket to Burnout City.

Remember, you're in this for the long haul. Pace yourself, be kind to yourself, and trust that by taking care of your own needs, you're also taking care of your podcast and your community. You've got this!

Incorporating podcasting into your work and personal life Let's face it, entrepreneurs, influencers, and every creative soul out there—you've got more balls in the air than a circus clown on a tightrope. How do you squeeze podcasting into that buzzing hive of activity? Well, it's simpler than teaching your grandma to upload pictures to Instagram. Imagine squeezing that podcasting lemon into your life smoothie, with a dash of planning and a sprinkle of creativity. For instance, you can turn your morning commute into a recording session. Picture yourself as the next Oprah, only you're suiting up in the car. Use hands-free devices—because, let's be real, nobody wants a podcast hosted by a hood ornament.

For those of you running businesses, turn those monotonous meetings into content havens. Meeting with a client? Why not interview them for your podcast? You'll get double the work done without missing a beat. Your personal life is fertile ground for podcast material too. Did little Timmy just learn to say "existentialism"? That's gold! Record those milestones, and you've got your next episode. This way, you get to podcast and still catch Timmy's off-key rendition of "Let It Go."

Finding the sweet spot between work, life, and your burgeoning podcast empire is like discovering the mythical unicorn. But guess what? Unicorns do exist. It's all about that elusive balance. Schedule blocks of time devoted solely to podcasting, much like you'd schedule dental appointments or spa days—except with fewer cavities and more fun. Leveraging tools like calendar apps to set reminders can keep you on track. You'll be less likely to skip recording sessions if Siri's breathing down your neck. And hey, nobody said you can't podcast from a bubble bath. Invest in water-proof equipment and get creative. Just make sure there's no background sound of toddlers dunking rubber ducks.

But here's the real secret sauce: make podcasting a non-negotiable part of your routine, like brushing your teeth or binging your favorite Netflix series. When you treat podcasting as an essential component of your life, rather than an optional hobby, you'll find ways to make it work, no matter how busy you are.

And don't forget the power of delegation and collaboration. You don't have to do everything yourself! Enlist the help of a virtual assistant, a co-host, or even a family member to help with tasks like scheduling, editing, or social media promotion. By sharing the load, you'll free up more time and energy to focus on the parts of podcasting that truly light you up.

Finally, remember that incorporating podcasting into your life is a journey, not a destination. There will be ups and downs, triumphs and challenges, and plenty of lessons learned along the way. Embrace the process, be patient with yourself, and trust that every step you take is bringing you closer to your podcasting goals.

And most importantly, have fun with it! Podcasting should be a source of joy, creativity, and connection, not just another item on your endless to-do list. When you approach it with a sense of playfulness and curiosity, you'll find that integrating it into your life becomes a natural, effortless process.

So, grab your microphone, your calendar, and your sense of adventure, and get ready to make podcasting a seamless part of your work and personal life. The world is waiting to hear your voice!

Reflection Questions:

1. What specific time-blocking strategies can you implement to ensure you're making time for podcasting amidst your other commitments?
2. What are some signs that you might be approaching burnout, and what self-care practices can you put in place to prevent it?

3. How can you leverage your existing work and personal experiences to generate content ideas for your podcast?

Congratulations, you've made it to the end of this chapter on balancing podcasting with other commitments! By now, you should have a solid toolkit of strategies for managing your time and energy, setting boundaries, avoiding burnout, and seamlessly integrating podcasting into your work and personal life.

But remember, balance is an ongoing practice, not a one-time achievement. It requires constant self-awareness, flexibility, and a willingness to adapt as your circumstances and priorities evolve. And that's okay! Embrace the ebb and flow of the journey, and trust that every challenge is an opportunity for growth and learning.

As you continue on your podcasting path, keep these key principles in mind:

1. Prioritize self-care and sustainability. You can't pour from an empty cup, so make sure you're taking care of your own needs first.
2. Be intentional with your time and energy. Focus on the tasks and activities that truly move the needle, and don't be afraid to say no to the rest.
3. Seek support and collaboration. You don't have to do it all alone! Build a team of allies, mentors, and collaborators who can help you achieve your goals.
4. Stay true to your passion and purpose. Remember why you started podcasting in the first place, and let that passion be your guiding light, even when things get tough.

And most importantly, celebrate your progress and successes along the way. Every episode published, every listener gained, every milestone reached – these are all testaments to your dedication, creativity, and courage. Take a moment to appreciate how far you've come, and use that momentum to propel you forward.

You've got this, podcasting superhero! Keep shining, keep creating, and keep inspiring the world with your unique voice and vision. The podcasting journey is a wild, wonderful ride – and we're so glad you're on it.

Exercise:

� Conduct a time audit of your current schedule and identify areas where you can prioritize podcasting tasks and responsibilities.

� Set realistic goals and deadlines for your podcasting projects and communicate them with your team or support system.

# Chapter 14: Guest Hosting and Being a Podcast Guest

Preparing for guest hosting opportunities Alright, folks, let's dive into the glamorous world of guest hosting. You've got the gig; now it's time to not just walk the walk but strut it like you're on a virtual catwalk. Rule number one: know your audience! Imagine walking into a room dressed to the nines, only to find everyone else in pajamas. Awkward, right? Whether you're addressing a room full of tech moguls, vibrant creators, or a mixed bag of entrepreneurial spirits, tailor your content and style to fit their groove. This isn't just about fitting in; it's about standing out in the best way possible.

Now, don't just wing it. Preparation is your best friend. Research the event or platform; understand the culture, the expectations, and the dos and don'ts. Think of it like learning the house rules before you dive into a heated game of Monopoly. Get to know the guest list – who's attending, why are they there, and what makes them tick. This way, you can drop those golden nuggets that keep people nodding enthusiastically and throwing thumbs-ups your way.

Content is king, queen, and the entire royal family when it comes to hosting. Start with a killer opener that grabs attention faster than a toddler grabs cookies. Think of a funny anecdote, an intriguing fact, or even a well-placed joke – something that shows you're not just a fancy face but a fancy face with personality. Keep your energy high and your content concise. Long-winded stories are great for grandma's porch, but here, you want punchy, engaging delivery that leaves them craving more.

Finally, practice makes perfect, but let's not aim for robotic perfection. Practice your lines, yes, but leave some room for spontaneity. You don't want to sound like you're reading from a teleprompter. Practice in front of a mirror, record yourself, or even better, grab a friend and go full-on performance mode. They can give you honest feedback and, let's be real, laugh at all your bad jokes so you can toss those out before the big day.

Quick tip: always have a glass of water handy. Nothing ruins a stellar performance like a sudden attack of the dry-throat monster. Plus, it gives you a moment to pause and gather your thoughts – or dramatically sip while the audience waits in suspense. Now go out there and host like the rockstar you were born to be!

And remember, guest hosting isn't just about showcasing your own brilliance; it's also about honoring the platform and the audience you've been entrusted with. Take the time to understand the show's mission, values, and unique voice, and find ways to align your own content and style with theirs. This isn't about stealing the spotlight; it's about creating a harmonious and engaging experience for everyone involved.

So, as you prepare for your guest hosting gig, keep these key principles in mind:

1. Know your audience and tailor your content accordingly.
2. Do your research and come prepared with killer content.
3. Practice, but leave room for spontaneity and authenticity.
4. Honor the platform and the audience by aligning with their values and voice.

And most importantly, have fun with it! Guest hosting is an incredible opportunity to flex your creative muscles, connect with new people, and make a lasting impact. So, embrace the challenge, bring your

A-game, and get ready to rock the virtual stage like the podcasting superstar you are!

Making a memorable impression as a podcast guest Let's be honest, making a killer first impression is a bit like trying to nail the perfect entrance at a party—while dodging the punch bowl and Aunt Margie's unsolicited advice. Step into the spotlight like you own it, even if you accidentally trip on the mic cord. Preparation Here is like plotting a heist, only you're stealing the hearts and minds of the listeners. Know the show's format, understand the host's quirks, and figure out who really tunes in. Are they entrepreneurs eager to unleash their next big idea or influencers hunting for their next viral post? Walk the walk, talk the talk, but most importantly, don't sound like you swallowed the corporate manual. Keep it real.

If making an impression is your game, then think of it as trying to leave the kind of impact that makes the mysterious disappearing act of Houdini look like a simple card trick. Engaging content isn't just about spilling your industry secrets; it's about weaving them into stories that make your fourth-grade campfire tales look like they were spun by an amateur. So, say goodbye to boring, irrelevant jargon and hello to quirky, memorable, and downright relatable exchanges. The goal? When the episode ends, the audience isn't just thinking, "Wow, they know their stuff," but "I want to hear more from them!" Punctuate your points with a sprinkle of humor, the touch of vulnerability, and a dash of dramatic flair - because the last thing you want is to sound like a robotic infomercial.

Ultimately, the secret sauce to being a standout podcast guest is a cocktail of preparedness, authenticity, and a captivating personality - served with a twist of wit. Don't just be a guest; be a showstopper. When the mic goes off, they should still be echoing your best moments. Be so unforgettable that when anyone asks the host about that amazing episode, the host doesn't blankly stare at their notes but immediately bursts into a recommendation, turning you into a podcast legend in your own right. Be prepared, be entertaining, and above all, be uniquely you. The rest will follow like a perfectly crafted podcast narrative.

But here's the thing: being a memorable podcast guest isn't just about stealing the show; it's also about being a gracious and respectful collaborator. Remember, you're a guest in someone else's home (or studio, in this case), and your job is to add value to their audience and their platform.

So, as you prepare to make your grand entrance, keep these key principles in mind:

1. Come prepared with engaging stories, valuable insights, and a dash of humor.
2. Be authentic, vulnerable, and relatable – no robotic infomercials allowed!
3. Respect the host, the audience, and the platform by being a gracious and collaborative guest.
4. Follow up after the episode airs to thank the host and engage with the audience.

And most importantly, have fun with it! Being a podcast guest is an incredible opportunity to share your message, connect with new people, and showcase your unique personality and expertise. So, embrace the challenge, bring your best self to the mic, and get ready to make a lasting impression on everyone who tunes in.

Trust us, with a little preparation, a lot of authenticity, and a sprinkle of that irresistible charm, you'll be the podcast guest that everyone can't stop talking about – for all the right reasons!

Maximizing the benefits of guest appearances Step right up, ladies, gents, and creative minds of all kinds! Ever thought that guest appearances were just free labor and exposure opportunities (cue eye roll)? Think again, my entrepreneurial enthusiasts! The trick to turning guest spots into golden opportunities is no secret—just a little laugh-inducing hustle and some strategic moves. First thing's first—think of guest spots as your runway debut. Whether you're strutting your stuff on a podcast, a blog, or even a YouTube channel, this is your moment to shine (cue Beyoncé's "Single Ladies"). Flaunt your expertise, sprinkle your quirky personality, and don't shy away from dropping some seriously valuable nuggets. Think of it as giving away free samples of your awesomeness; people love freebies, and before you know it, they'll be flocking to your main gig.

Now, let's talk leverage, because we're all about working smarter, not harder (unless you're a fan of working yourself into an early nap). Once you've wowed the audience, don't just leave them dangling; reel them in slowly but surely. Craft an irresistible call-to-action that directs them back to your own turf. Maybe it's a free e-book, an exclusive webinar, or even a cheeky discount code. Just make sure it's something that makes following you a no-brainer. And while you're at it, put a little time into those post-appearance follow-ups. Send a thank-you note, share the appearance on your social media, and even consider a quick recap blog post. Not only does it show you're grateful (and we totally are—we swear), but it keeps the conversation alive and well.

Let's get cheeky and talk about turning these guest appearances into genuine growth vehicles. You're not just a flash in the pan—you're the whole darn fireworks show. Analyze what worked, what didn't, and tweak your approach with each new opportunity. If one particular type of guest spot brought in heaps of traffic or tons of new followers, double down on that format. On the flip side, if something fizzled (hey, it happens to the best of us), adapt and improve. Keep track of metrics, whether it's website visits, follower counts, or even the number of giggle-snorts you got during a podcast interview. The goal is to make each appearance a stepping stone to greater success.

And here's the kicker. Practice makes perfect, and humor makes it memorable. Keep that balance between usefulness and light-hearted fun, and you'll not only educate but also entertain. Yes, cats, and baby pics will always rule the internet, but you, with your savvy know-how and charm, can give them a run for their money. So suit up, guests of honor, and let's turn those guest spots into grand opportunities!

But wait, there's more! Maximizing the benefits of guest appearances isn't just about what happens during and immediately after the episode; it's also about the long-term relationships you build and the opportunities you create for ongoing collaboration and mutual support.

So, as you navigate the exciting world of guest appearances, keep these key principles in mind:

1. Treat each guest spot as an opportunity to provide genuine value and showcase your unique expertise and personality.
2. Create compelling calls-to-action that encourage listeners to engage with you beyond the episode.
3. Follow up with the host and the audience to keep the conversation going and build lasting relationships.
4. Analyze your metrics and adjust your approach based on what works and what doesn't.
5. Look for opportunities to collaborate with the host and other guests in the future.

And most importantly, have fun with it! Guest appearances are an incredible way to expand your reach, build your authority, and connect with new people who share your passions and interests. So, embrace the challenge, bring your best self to the mic, and get ready to turn those guest spots into a launching pad for your podcasting success.

Who knows? With a little luck, a lot of hustle, and a whole bunch of irresistible charm, you might just become the go-to podcast guest that everyone can't wait to have on their show. And that, my friends, is what we call a podcasting win-win!

Reflection Questions:

1. What are some unique ways you can research and prepare for a guest hosting opportunity to ensure you deliver maximum value to the audience?
2. How can you infuse your own personality and story-telling style into your guest appearances while still respecting the host's platform and audience?
3. What specific calls-to-action or follow-up strategies can you implement to turn one-time guest appearances into ongoing opportunities for growth and collaboration?

And there you have it, folks – the ultimate guide to guest hosting and being a podcast guest! By now, you should have a solid understanding of how to prepare for guest hosting opportunities, make a memorable impression as a podcast guest, and maximize the benefits of your guest appearances.

But remember, the real magic happens when you put these strategies into action and start showing up as your most authentic, valuable, and engaging self. Whether you're stepping into the spotlight as a guest host or sharing your expertise as a guest on someone else's show, always keep your focus on providing value, building relationships, and having fun along the way.

And don't be afraid to step outside your comfort zone and try new things! The world of podcasting is vast and full of endless possibilities, and you never know where your next guest appearance might lead. So, say yes to those opportunities, put in the work to prepare and follow up, and trust that your unique voice and perspective have the power to make a real impact on the lives of others.

And most importantly, never forget why you started podcasting in the first place. Whether you're in it to build your business, share your message, or simply connect with like-minded people, always stay true to your purpose and your passion. Because when you lead with your heart and your authenticity, you'll attract the right opportunities, the right audiences, and the right relationships to help you grow and thrive.

So, go forth and conquer the podcasting world, one guest appearance at a time! We can't wait to hear all about your adventures and celebrate your success along the way. Happy podcasting!

Exercise:

� Reach out to 3 podcasts in your niche and pitch yourself as a potential guest, highlighting your expertise and unique perspective.

� Prepare a list of talking points and potential questions for your next guest appearance.

# Chapter 15: The Future of Podcasting

Trends and innovations in the podcasting industry If you haven't noticed, podcasts are the new black. Everyone and their pet iguana seem to have one. But what's really shaking things up in the audio world? Two words: true crime. Yes, it turns out that tales of murder and mayhem are like catnip for listeners. But don't fret; if dissecting grim tales isn't your thing, there's always room for self-improvement shows. Just imagine your listeners transforming from mere mortals into productive powerhouses, all thanks to your dulcet tones. Oh, and did we mention celebrity-hosted podcasts? If you can pull a famous face into your project, you're basically golden.

On the tech front, gone are the days when a podcast was a mere phoned-in chat. Now, we're talking about fancy stuff like 3D audio, making listeners feel like they're smack dab in the middle of a buzzing rainforest or a bustling market. AI is also creeping in, doing everything from editing to scriptwriting. This means less time sweating over "ums" and "ahs" and more time doing what you do best: being fabulous. And let's not forget interactive podcasts, where the audience gets to choose their own auditory adventure. Just make sure you don't end up on a cliffhanger with no way out.

Lastly, a word to the wise: don't be a dinosaur. Embrace these trends and tech updates like they're the last cookie in the jar. Incorporate flashy features, sprinkle in some celebrity dazzle if you can, and for heaven's sake, diversify your content. That way, whether your listener is a wannabe detective, a self-help junkie, or just someone trying to evade boredom, you've got them covered. Now, go turn that microphone into your new best friend and make something binge-worthy.

But wait, there's more! The future of podcasting isn't just about flashy tech and celebrity cameos; it's also about the growing importance of authenticity and community-building. As the podcasting landscape becomes more crowded and competitive, listeners are craving hosts and shows that feel genuine, relatable, and engaged with their audience.

So, as you navigate the exciting world of podcasting trends and innovations, don't forget to stay true to yourself and your unique voice. Embrace new technologies and formats that align with your brand and your message, but always keep your focus on creating content that resonates with your listeners on a deep, personal level.

And remember, building a loyal, engaged community around your podcast is just as important as staying on top of the latest trends. Foster meaningful connections with your listeners through social media, email newsletters, and in-person events. Create opportunities for your audience to interact with you and with each other, and always be responsive to their feedback and ideas.

At the end of the day, the future of podcasting belongs to those who are willing to experiment, take risks, and put their heart and soul into creating something truly special. So, don't be afraid to think outside the box, try new things, and let your creativity run wild. The podcasting world is waiting for you to make your mark!

Predictions for the future of podcast consumption So, you've jumped on the podcast bandwagon, huh? Well, buckle up, because the podcasting world is evolving faster than you can say "download and subscribe." In the near future, expect podcasting to be more ubiquitous than caffeine in a co-working space. Imagine your smart fridge recommending you a podcast just as it nags you to buy more oat milk. That's where we're headed!

If you thought binge-watching was just for Netflix, think again. Podcast consumers are going to develop some serious binging habits. Imagine a weekend dedicated solely to the latest murder mystery podcast, with intermissions only for snack breaks and existential musings. Listeners will demand not only quantity but a high level of quality. This means, entrepreneurs and influencers, you'd better sharpen your storytelling skills unless you want your podcast to be the audio equivalent of dot-matrix printer noise.

Speaking of quantity, let's talk about niche content. One size does not fit all, especially in earbuds. Expect highly specialized content that caters to the most unique interests. There will be podcasts about underwater basket weaving techniques, ancient alien theories, and even the daily lives of pet hamsters. As a creative outlet, this opens the door for you to dive into your quirkiest passions and find an audience equally as quirky. Everyone's a weirdo these days; embrace it!

Another big change? Say goodbye to traditional ad reads and hello to dynamic ad insertion. This means the days of podcasters awkwardly segwaying from a ghost story to a mattress commercial are numbered. Soon, technology will seamlessly drop in ads tailored to the listener's interests and behaviors. Ads will feel less like ads and more like recommendations from a friend who just happens to know you need a new blender. This is gold for you influencers out there—you can focus on your narrative without selling your soul (or your podcast) to sponsorship fatigue.

Lastly, social interaction around podcasts is going to skyrocket. Think real-time comments, live podcasts with audience participation, and discussion forums that rival those of the most active fandoms. Podcast consumption will no longer be a solitary experience where your only interaction is nodding along invisibly. Start thinking about how you can engage your listeners, create communities, and maybe even spark some good old-fashioned internet debates. If nothing else, you'll have plenty of content for a follow-up episode!

So, there you have it. The future of podcasting is as limitless as your imagination—full of innovation, interaction, and perhaps a tad bit of craziness. If you're ready to ride this wave, focus on storytelling, embrace niche topics, and prepare for a world where ads blend like a chameleon into your content. Now go hit that record button and be a part of the revolution!

But here's the thing: as exciting as all these predictions are, the future of podcast consumption ultimately comes down to one thing – the listener. As a podcaster, your job is to create content that not only entertains and informs but also forges a deep, lasting connection with your audience.

So, as you ponder the possibilities of the podcasting landscape, always keep your listener at the forefront of your mind. What are their needs, their desires, their pain points? How can you create content that not only meets them where they are but also helps them grow, learn, and evolve?

And don't be afraid to get personal. Share your own stories, struggles, and triumphs. Be vulnerable, be authentic, and be unapologetically yourself. Because in a world of endless content and countless distractions, it's the podcasts that feel like a genuine conversation between friends that will stand the test of time.

So, whether you're diving into true crime, exploring niche topics, or experimenting with interactive formats, always remember that your listener is the heart and soul of your podcast. Treat them with respect, gratitude, and a whole lot of love, and you'll be well on your way to creating a show that not only survives but thrives in the ever-evolving world of podcasting.

Adapting to changes and staying ahead of the curve As an entrepreneur or influencer, you're like a chameleon in a room full of new wallpaper. Industries change faster than a toddler's mood, and for survival, you must adapt. Picture this: one day, your business is the talk of the town, the next, it's as relevant as a Blockbuster store. Staying updated with the latest trends isn't just a good idea—it's a matter of life and revenue. Careers in tech, fashion, marketing, or any creative outlet demand your Sherlock Holmes hat. If Instagram decides that cat photos are out and llama selfies are in, guess what? You better grab a llama. The key is to continually educate yourself. Attend workshops, webinars, and even eavesdrop at coffee shops if it helps you catch the buzz.

Innovation isn't just building the next flying car; it's about being forward-thinking. Take the wheel on small, practical improvements in your everyday operations. Imagine you're running an igloo business in the Sahara—clearly, you need to think differently. Reevaluate practices when they become as outdated as fashion from the early 2000s. Create brainstorming sessions with your team, and don't dismiss any idea, no matter how insanely great, to borrow a phrase from our tech overlord Steve Jobs. Wacky might just be wonderful. Use feedback loops to understand your audience. Are they laughing at your latest post because it's genuinely funny or because your hashtag game looks like your grandma tried using Twitter? Adapt and enhance based on real-time reactions.

If you think just reading about innovation will keep you ahead, then bless your optimism. Practically implementing your grand ideas is where the magic happens. Just like your yoga instructor harps on about aligning your chakras, align your strategies. Test new ideas patiently but consistently—it's like fishing; not every cast catches a big one, but perseverance brings results. Metrics and analytics may sound as fun as watching paint dry, but they're crucial. Keep an eye on data; it tells a story clearer than any crystal ball. Whether you're catering to women,

men or people looking for a creative outlet, strike when the iron is hot and adjust swiftly if things start fizzling out.

Here's a nugget of wisdom: change is the only constant, so might as well get comfy with it. The secret sauce to staying relevant is to always expect the unexpected. Your creativity must be like a Swiss Army Knife, ready to pivot from one task to another. So, stay nimble, stay curious, and keep your eye on the prize—the ever-evolving, elusive, yet incredibly rewarding goal of staying ahead of the curve.

But here's the catch: adapting to change and staying ahead of the curve isn't just about chasing the latest shiny object or jumping on every trending bandwagon. It's about having a deep understanding of your industry, your audience, and yourself, and using that knowledge to make strategic, purposeful decisions.

So, as you navigate the ever-changing landscape of podcasting (and entrepreneurship in general), remember to stay grounded in your values, your mission, and your unique voice. Don't be afraid to experiment and take risks, but always do so with intention and integrity.

And most importantly, never stop learning. Seek out mentors, collaborators, and communities that challenge you to grow and evolve. Attend conferences, read books and articles, and engage in meaningful conversations with people who have different perspectives and experiences than you. The more you expose yourself to new ideas and ways of thinking, the better equipped you'll be to adapt to whatever changes come your way.

Remember, staying ahead of the curve isn't about predicting the future; it's about being open, agile, and ready to embrace it when it arrives. So, keep your mind sharp, your heart open, and your podcasting skills on point, and you'll be well on your way to making your mark in this exciting, ever-evolving industry.

Reflection Questions:

1. Which podcasting trends or innovations are you most excited to explore or implement in your own show?
2. How can you start preparing now for the predicted changes in podcast consumption and listener behavior?
3. What steps can you take to continuously educate yourself and stay ahead of the curve in the podcasting industry?

And there you have it, folks – a sneak peek into the future of podcasting! By now, your mind is probably buzzing with ideas, possibilities, and maybe even a few nervous butterflies. But fear not, my fellow podcasting adventurers – the future is bright, and you're already well on your way to making your mark in this exciting, ever-evolving industry.

As you ponder the trends, predictions, and strategies we've explored in this chapter, remember that the true key to success in podcasting (and in life) is to stay true to yourself, your values, and your unique voice. Don't get so caught up in chasing the latest shiny object that you lose sight of what makes you, you.

Instead, focus on creating content that resonates with your audience, nurturing genuine connections and communities, and always, always, always putting your heart and soul into everything you do. Because in the end, it's not about the fancy tech, the celebrity guests, or the flashy marketing – it's about the magic that happens when you share your authentic self with the world.

So, as you step boldly into the future of podcasting, armed with all the insights and inspiration from this book, know that you have everything you need to succeed already inside of you. Your creativity, your passion, your unique perspective – these are the tools that will help you navigate whatever changes and challenges come your way.

And remember, you're not alone on this journey. The podcasting community is filled with incredible, supportive, and like-minded individuals who are all rooting for your success. So, don't be afraid to reach out, collaborate, and lean on others when you need a little extra encouragement or guidance.

The future of podcasting is yours for the taking, my friends. So, go forth and create, innovate, and inspire – the world is waiting to hear your voice!

Exercise:

� Research and identify 2-3 emerging trends or technologies in the podcasting industry that you could potentially incorporate into your show.

� Set a goal for your podcast growth and development over the next 6-12 months and create an action plan to achieve it.

## Conclusion: Unleashing Your Inner Podcasting Rockstar

Well, well, well. Look at you, you podcasting prodigy! You've journeyed through the ups, downs, and sideways of this wild podcasting adventure, and now you're standing on the precipice of greatness, ready to take the audio world by storm.

Throughout this book, we've covered everything from finding your unique voice and niche to navigating the technical tango of recording and editing. We've delved into the art of crafting irresistible content, building a loyal audience, and even monetizing your passion. And along the way, we've had a few laughs, a few tears (mostly from laughter), and countless "a-ha!" moments.

But here's the thing: this is just the beginning. The world of podcasting is constantly evolving, and there's always more to learn, more to experiment with, and more to create. So, as you step boldly into your podcasting future, remember to stay curious, stay open, and stay true to yourself.

Keep putting yourself out there, even when it feels scary. Keep pushing yourself to try new things, even when it feels uncomfortable. And keep showing up, even when you're not sure anyone is listening. Because the truth is, someone is always listening. And your voice, your message, and your unique perspective have the power to change lives, one episode at a time.

As you continue on your podcasting journey, remember to celebrate your victories, learn from your failures, and never, ever stop believing in the magic of your own voice. You've got this, you podcasting rockstar. Now go out there and make some noise!

## Podcasting Cheat Sheet:

1. Define your niche and target audience
2. Invest in quality equipment and software
3. Plan and outline your episodes in advance
4. Record in a quiet space with good acoustics
5. Edit for clarity, flow, and optimal sound quality
6. Launch with 3-5 episodes and consistent branding
7. Promote across multiple channels and platforms
8. Engage with your audience and build community
9. Monetize through sponsorships, affiliate marketing, or products
10. Continuously improve and evolve your content and style

## Don't miss out!

Visit the website below and you can sign up to receive emails whenever Jennifer Boyte publishes a new book. There's no charge and no obligation.

https://books2read.com/r/B-A-RHVLB-FRSID

BOOKS 2 READ

Connecting independent readers to independent writers.

Did you love *Should I Start A Podcast? What About!!??! A Step by Step Guide to Achieving Your Podcasting Dream*? Then you should read *Procrastination No More: The Ultimate Guide To Boosting Productivity And Achieving Your Goals*[1] by Jennifer Boyte!

[2]

Procrastination to Productivity is a transformative, step-by-step guide for overcoming the pervasive challenge of procrastination and unlocking your innate potential for extraordinary achievement and providing a comprehensive roadmap for cultivating the mindset, habits, and routines of highly effective, consistently productive individuals.

This book is a must-read for anyone seeking to break free from the shackles of procrastination, harness their full creative potential, and accelerate their progress toward their most ambitious personal and

1. https://books2read.com/u/bP8RMR

2. https://books2read.com/u/bP8RMR

professional goals. With clarity, compassion, and infectious enthusiasm you will be guided through a profound process of self-discovery and empowerment. You will be equipped with the tools and insights they need to conquer overwhelm, master their time and energy, and create a life of boundless productivity, prosperity, and fulfillment.

Whether you're an entrepreneur, executive, student, or anyone struggling to turn their dreams into reality, "Procrastination to Productivity" offers a clear, compelling path forward. Prepare to be inspired, challenged, and transformed as you embark upon this exhilarating journey of self-actualization and discover the limitless potential that awaits you on the other side of procrastination.

# Also by Jennifer Boyte

Procrastination No More: The Ultimate Guide To Boosting Productivity And Achieving Your Goals
Goal Mastery: A Practical Guide To Setting And Achieving Your Dreams
Should I Start A Podcast? What About!!??! A Step by Step Guide to Achieving Your Podcasting Dream

www.ingramcontent.com/pod-product-compliance
Lightning Source LLC
LaVergne TN
LVHW012113160826
845678LV00014B/3065

* 9 7 9 8 2 2 4 3 7 7 9 5 4 *